# CLOSE ENCOUNTERS

# OF THE GOD KIND

*Exploring the Infinite Riches of God*

by
Adele Hooker

PublishAmerica
Baltimore

First printing

At the specific preference of the author, PublishAmerica allowed this work to remain exactly as the author intended, verbatim, without editorial input.

ISBN: 1-4241-6333-1
PUBLISHED BY PUBLISHAMERICA, LLLP
www.publishamerica.com
Baltimore

Printed in the United States of America

# About the Author

Adele Hooker is a retired school teacher. She is a pastor's wife, counselor and speaker. She has three other books in print: *How To Find God In Everyday Living* by PublishAmerica, *Prayer and Other God Stuff* and *The Gwinner Family Saga*, self published.

Her hobbies are poetry and non-fiction writing. Her poems are featured in seven different international anthologies of poetry, including "The International Who's Who of Poetry" (2005) by *The International Library of Poetry*.

She and her husband Samuel of sixty-five years, are both ministers. They have three children with families, six grandchildren and four great-grandchildren.

Besides her family, Adele's special interests are prayer and helping people find God's best for their lives.

"This is why I write," Adele says.

# Contents

# MIRACLES

***** 

ALBERT EINSTEIN SAID
THERE ARE TWO WAYS
TO LIVE LIFE: LIKE
NOTHING IS A MIRACLE.
OR
EVERYTHING IS A MIRACLE.

## DEDICATION

***

I'm happy to dedicate this book of miracles
to the miracle of my life,
my husband,
Reverend Samuel E. Hooker.
We have been blessed together
with a wonderful family and sixty-five years
of marriage and pastoral ministry.

# APPRECIATION

\*\*\*

No way could this book exist
without the gifts of many
dedicated friends.
Graciously you gave your miracle stories,
whether verbally or written.
To each of you
I give grateful hugs.
Hugs also to Judy Guyton,
an amazing proof reader.

# Foreword

Adele Hooker's book, *Close Encounters of the God Kind* shadows her perpetual-motion-life. "What you see is what you get." She is what she writes in every energetic word: a mover, with friendships unlimited and energy boundless. This work is probably unintentionally a wide ranging expose of herself as a pastor's wife and helpmate, never content with the role of a voiceless onlooker.

Her "given" family, equally devoted disciples, German-Russian immigration by way of Canada, escaped from tyranny—that's a story in itself, which she has written.

Her book reflects her wide ranging friendships from corporation chiefs to every creature, even former hoboes, telling their stories of miracle beyond the ken of non-believers. Her life itself is miracle after miracle. No surprise then that she writes about God's graces and has invested her adult life helping others shore up their own God presence, adding authentication of her own report.

Her faith and energy awes and frightens me, makes me wonder if such will fit around even Christian writing. Surprisingly, it fits like a glove. I become immersed as in a flood that turns kindly with reading.

Adele's husband, Pastor Sam, becomes a strong truss in her structure of faith by his own recovery from childhood disaster—with lifelong damage, injuries fraught with the tenacity of a Missouri mule, the strength of Goliath, and the purpose of a David.

This book reaches for faith in corners heretofore hidden even to close confidants of her co-miracle-revealers.

Adele was a high school English teacher in addition to pastor's wife and partner. As an author she has been recognized by national associations.

This one has known Adele and Pastor Sam for over half a century, in fact, made a midnight call from Oregon to them many years ago, telling of the Woodstock Church Pulpit Committee's request that they pray about accepting what we believed was a "God Call" to pastor this church.

A hand grenade was dropped into their lives, "asking them to leave a people they loved, a community that had become the fabric of their souls." ....agony, not anticipated, asked for, nor wanted.... upheaval....

They came.... with prayer and fasting, rumbling and agony, to engage in a long term, highly successful pastorate, doubling and tripling the size of the church.

Adele is remembered for personally faith-cementing a clutch of seeking souls labeled "The Strugglers," probably a term indicating the effort in digging the well-of-faith. The power of faith and devotion are reflected as she talks of God's extra touch in lives. Few would be more qualified to write and assemble these many accounts of faith effort.

Dr. Haughton B. Lee, Retired
College Professor,
Superintendent of Schools

# Introduction

Webster says a miracle is "an event in the physical world that surpasses all known human or natural powers and is ascribed to divine or supernatural cause; a wonder; a marvel."

If this is so, then we surely have here a museum full of these exotic entities. You, the reader, are invited to vicariously experience these marvelous wonders.

Far and near, I searched to gathered these sixty-two stories and I've thrilled to goose bumps working with them. It has been an honor as well as a pleasure to interview the recipients of these interventions of the divine.

Personally, I have had multiple experiences which I could not attribute to any other source than my loving, living Lord and Saviour Jesus Christ.

Early in my adult life I was fortunate enough to have sickness and trouble beyond my ability to cope. It drove me to seek the deep heart of Jesus. I was blessed to have a mother who prayed. Although that did not assure me of God's help when I called. Yet, by seeing her prayer life I knew God was there. I just needed to seek him until I got myself out of the way enough to let him find me.

Many of these stories are of my own experience. In these my by-line is marked A. H.

A sparse few of my stories appear in another book. I feel their vital truths deserve further circulation.

Most stories are of other people. Some are written by the persons experiencing them. Others are as told to me. In these you will see my writing style. But all facts and information are accurate as related to me by the individual who experienced the miracle.

Then come with me, and together let us explore a small portion of the incredible, infinite riches of our God.

Adele Hooker

# CHAPTER 1

# Saved—A Big New Beautiful Red Motorcycle

*Kim Raichl*

Joshua, my six-year-old son and I were driving on highway I-5 from Astoria, Oregon to Seattle, Washington in my purple, 2000, Dodge Neon. All the way we were singing with Christian tapes. We just passed Tacoma, Washington, still singing our praise songs, when I noticed a young man riding up on a big, bright red, new motorcycle. He was decked out from head to toe in new-looking, black cycling gear. It appeared he just bought a roaring-big-bike and an outfit to go with it.

I was in the commuter lane at the left side of the highway, going about sixty miles an hour. The cyclist, coming up fast on my right, was going seventy or more. What neither of us could see was, the car ahead of him straddled a large piece of lumber, a 4X4. When I saw it, quickly I veered to the left to give the biker as much room as possible while nervously keeping my eyes on the guard rail to avoid scraping it. At the speed the biker was coming I thought, It's impossible! He can't miss that!

He didn't.

I cried out, "God, save him!"

He hit the 4X4, shot up into the air and flew downward toward my lane in front of me. I gripped the steering wheel with white knuckles, knowing I was going to run him over. Instead of landing in my lane, he flipped and whirled in such a way as to land in his own lane, on both wheels, moving straight and steady forward, right beside my car.

"How could he do it?" my shocked and confused mind shouted.

"No way!" I answered myself.

For several yards the rider stayed next to me. He looked into my car and directly at me. His wild, baffled face defied description. I opened my eyes wide, stretched my face in a grimace of fear and awe that said, "Wow! You're alive! God saved you!"

Then I gave him a hearty thumbs up. I didn't know what else to do.

He sped off at the next exit.

Maybe he's going off to thank God for saving his life, I thought.

I wish I had followed him and asked if he knew God gave him a miracle. I knew, and I was thanking God all the way on that I didn't have to live with the horrendous, life-plaguing memory of killing a man—or even seeing him smashed on the pavement in front of me. I didn't care a whit that God saved his big, new, red motorcycle. In fact, I was seething-mad at the thing for being so dangerous.

It took me a while to realize—Hey! God saved us too!

# CHAPTER 2

# Singing "Amazing Grace"

## *Kurt Salierno*

I stuttered so bad when I was a kid, I couldn't say one fluid sentence. I had very few friends and I was voted the most unlikely to succeed in my senior class. The good that came out of it—I sure can sympathize with hurting people.

Jesus was my best friend. He and I developed a close relationship. I walked down the streets of my home town, Visalia, California, talking out loud to Jesus. And I heard him talk to me, too. People didn't understand. They thought I was mentally challenged.

I attended a small church congregation and I was active in it. One day I told my pastor I felt God wanted me to go into the ministry. He chuckled and said, "Kurt, you can't even talk."

I didn't know just what to do with the pastor's response, but I said, "I don't know how it's going to happen, except that I can trust God with all my heart. Moses told God, "No." I want to tell God, "Yes.""

Pastor Roper invited me to speak at an evening service. When the people heard that "that stuttering kid" was going to preach, they came out in full force. The usual group of ten or twelve ballooned out to fill the church sanctuary. It was the most ever to attend an evening service in our church.

Of course, I was terrified, but my trust was in God and I was willing for him to do whatever he wanted with me. I'd already been humiliated many times, one more would be OK. Surprisingly, I didn't stutter. I delivered the message I felt God gave me and never stuttered once—the first time in my entire life. I pinched myself to see if I was dreaming. And then I realized, I couldn't be. I even stutter in my dreams.

At the end of my sermon, Pastor came up to me and said, "Wow, you are called of God!"

Financially the church helped me attend Warner Pacific College in Portland, Oregon.

Here I got in trouble.

I understood the street people who had no friends and didn't know that Jesus would be their friend. I wanted to help them. So I spent my evenings and sometimes all night on the downtown streets of Portland, befriending the outcasts. I could feel their pain. I hurt for them. Unlike these homeless people, I had a family and a church that loved me. Best of all, I had a friend, Jesus. He was a friend who was always with me. Even though I often felt lonely, I knew I was never alone. I wanted these outcasts to know Jesus, too.

After a bit of a hassle, the college allowed me to continue my street ministry, but I had to move off campus. A good pastor and church took me in. I lived in the attic of the Rockwood Church of God and became their associate pastor. This allowed me to continue my work with the homeless, telling them the Psalm 139 Principle: "You are not a mistake. You are wonderfully and beautifully made. God loves you."

In college I met my wonderful wife.

Now I'm a minister in Atlanta, Georgia. I spend many of my evenings and nights making friends with the street people who are battling drugs and alcohol. I tell them about the one who can help them, the one who cares when nobody else does. I tell them I care, too.

My biggest miracle is being in the ministry and able to talk to people about Jesus—Jesus, the one I love more than life. He's been my closest friend. He gave me a deeply satisfying life purpose. He is also my protector. On the streets at night with many angry, hurting, doped-out-of-their-minds people I've really seen his miraculous power. Three incidents come to mind

One night someone tried to kill me with a knife. Even with two hands he couldn't get the knife into my shirt. While he was doing it, I prayed out loud for him. He dropped the knife and ran.

Another man tried to stab me in the back with his pocket knife. The Holy Spirit prevented the knife from penetrating. Frustrated, the man threw the knife at me and ran off.

One homeless man tried to shoot me. He stole a gun, shot somebody else, killed them and came to kill me. He put the gun to my head and pulled the trigger. Again and again, six times, he pulled the trigger.

Frozen with fear, I couldn't do anything but pray. Frustrated, the man thought the bullets were bad and threw them on the ground to use new ones. He was about to shoot me again but other homeless guys alerted the police who came. The police checked the gun and the used bullets. They shot fine. "There's nothing wrong with this gun or the bullets," the officer said. "Take the bullets to remind you that there's someone greater watching over you."

On the streets we see miracles happen every week. Lives are changed all the time. It's God. He said he'd show his strength through our weakness.

I have a speech impediment and I struggled through high school and college. But that helps me to relate to the guys on the streets who are struggling: homeless, helpless and poor. So now I get to sing "Amazing grace how sweet the sound" with many redeemed street people.

# CHAPTER 3

# Marilyn's Brush with Death

## *Dale Warman*

It was May 1, 2002 at two a.m. that my wife, Marilyn, woke up with a terrible headache. I brought her aspirin. When she started to drink the water she convulsed and vomited blood. I knew we had a problem.

Immediately I got her into clothes and helped her into the car. The hospital is less than five minutes from us. It would take longer if I called 911. On the way she was already talking out of her head.

At emergency I jumped out of the car, hollering, "Help! Help! Help!"

Two male nurses ran out with a gurney. They took Marilyn straight into emergency. Immediately the attendants worked to stabilize her and called the brain surgeon. They recorded a "cat scan" and other information for the doctor when he got there. It took the surgeon about thirty minutes to get to the hospital. While he was coming, I called Doug, our older son, and asked him to call our two other children, Sharon and Ron, which he did. Sharon called our pastors, Rev. Marvel and Rev. Burch and alerted our church prayer chain.

Our children, the pastors, and the surgeon all arrived about the same time.

The surgeon looked at the report and at Marilyn then called us together. He said to me, "Your wife has bled so badly that it's amazing she is still breathing. Ninety percent of the people who have a front lobed aneurysm don't even make it to the hospital alive." He didn't recommend surgery, saying, "Very few people who do make it here survive the seven or eight hours of grueling surgery. If she survived that, she'd probably be a vegetable."

We talked about surgery and my children and I thought we should have a second opinion. We asked that his superior and he talk with us together.

Frankly, the doctor looked so young I thought he was in his early twenties. I asked him, "How old are you?" He said, "I'm forty-two." I felt better about him then.

After we visited with the two surgeons, I asked that we be given time alone to talk things over. Pastor Marvel lead us in prayer, asking God's counsel for our decision. After prayer and more discussion we felt we should go ahead with the surgery in spite of the poor odds. Patty, our daughter-in-law, asked if we could lay hands on the doctors and pray for them. The doctors agreed. We circled around them and Pastor Burch prayed a strong prayer for God to intercede and to guide the minds and hands of the surgeons.

We told them to go forward. Immediately they took Marilyn into the operating room. One of the doctors situated the family in a separate room and told us surgery would take six to eight hours.

We called friends, asking for prayer. We called church prayer chains and the "Live Week End" office to put Marilyn on the prayer chain. From here a call went to Dave Coolidge in Anderson, Indiana. He alerted our denomination's "International Church of God Prayer Chain." The message went to missionaries and churches around the world.

(Throughout the weeks, we received at least eighty emails from people everywhere telling us they were praying for Marilyn.)

Throughout the hours of anxious waiting we were in constant prayer. After seven hours, Dr. Rouquest came to the family room and told us the surgery went as well as could be expected. But there was a lot of damage because of the excessive bleeding. Also, Marilyn went into coma during the operation.

Up in the hairline they cut the full length across the forehead and laid that part of Marilyn's skull back. Dr. Rouquest later explained, "It took twelve staples to put her skull back together."

After surgery they moved Marilyn to ICU. We were allowed to go in to her only two at a time. For two or three days the whole family stayed at the hospital and hoped and prayed for God's good news. Finally we realized we needed a plan. We decided to take our vigils in shifts. For four hours at a time two family members sat with Marilyn around the clock. She was never alone. Always she was prayed with, talked to and encouraged to win the battle.

The daily reports were that Marilyn was constantly deteriorating. Finally, after eighteen days of deterioration, the family was told she had only a couple days to live.

"We're going to move you all into a private room so you can have family time with her," the doctor said. He recommended we remove the life supports. A hospice person and the hospital chaplain were directed to our room. They spoke of making plans for Marilyn's final day.

We called another family-pastor conference. After much discussion and prayer we agreed to disconnect Marilyn from all life supports. We reasoned, "If God is going to heal her, he doesn't need life supports to do it."

Eighteen hours after the supports were removed, Patty was sitting with Marilyn. She came out to the hall where we were all waiting and said, "Something spooky is going on in there. Mom's mumbling."

Quickly I went in and leaned over my Sweetheart and said, "Are you awake, Honey?"

In a voice raspy from the tubes and with vocal cords that had not been in use for eighteen days, she whispered, "I hurt all over."

We all started laughing, crying, shouting, praising God. The celebration was wild!

Nurses came running to see the happy commotion. With great surprise, they too celebrated. They had fallen in love with this needy patient they tended devotedly for four and a half weeks.

The family agreed that it appeared God was waiting for us to disconnect the supports so he could show his mighty power and his great love for us.

Now, here we were at the start of a long, arduous journey toward recovery. Marilyn was paralyzed. The doctors told us to think in terms of marathon and not sprint. Even getting her to sit up in bed took great effort on everyone's part. Marilyn had to be a warrior. She had hard battles to fight before the war would be over. But fight her battles she did. And that without losing her smile and kind disposition. The nurses now really fell in love with this gentle, spiritual champion as they saw her struggle so enduringly to gain back her abilities. For three and a half months she was in strenuous hospital therapy. Finally, on September seventeenth, she was released to come home.

Marilyn entered the house with a walker. All the family and a host of friends were there to celebrate her home coming. We applauded her for working so hard to accomplish this great triumph and we gave thanks to God for his marvelous gift—the miracle of a second life.

Her therapy continued.

In ten months she went from paralysis, to wheelchair, to walker, to cane, to near-normal walking.

Still now, at the time of this writing, Marilyn spends four days a week in therapy. She walks two miles, does weight lifting and aerobics of different kinds. All her faculties have returned except some short term memory. We're trusting God for this, too, to return!

Four weeks after Marilyn came home she and I started practicing with our church's "Singing Christmas Tree." It was the thirtieth year the First Church of God in Vancouver, Washington put on this special concert. Marilyn and I were in the first one. There were ten, ninety-minute concerts. Marilyn handled them as well as any of the other one hundred members.

At Easter time Marilyn and I took an Easter Lilly up to the hospital to put into the nurses' station in gratitude for those who tended Marilyn so lovingly. Oh! how excited they all were to see Marilyn—well and walking. One nurse told us, "That first night, I wrote in my log, 'Marilyn won't make it through the night. No hope.'"

On May first, one year after her surgery, Marilyn led the opening devotions at the "Live Spiritual Renewal Rally" in Rome, Italy. She and I sang a duet, the Gaither's song, "You Can't Out Love the Lord," And, too, in gratitude for the many, many prayers, our hearts are still singing, "You Can't Out Love the Love of God's People."

This past month, June, 2003, Marilyn and her sister, Carol, served coffee in the "Live Week End" tent at the International Church of God Convention. Here many people told Marilyn they had prayed for her.

She thanked them with great gratitude.

# CHAPTER 4

# My Spiritual Jewels

## *"Just Betty"*

My name is Betty. I walk the Clackamas Town Center Mall in Portland, Oregon where Adele Hooker walks each weekday morning. Adele told me she was collecting miracles. I said, "I have two jewels—unforgettable!"

"I've got to have them," she said.

We stopped in the middle of our walk and I told her my stories.

### JEWEL I
### WINDS OF THE SPIRIT

The first miracle happened twenty years ago when my semi-invalid mother-in-law was living with us. The three of us, Mother, my husband Bill, and I came home from the beach at Lincoln City, Oregon. It was a cold, winter night. We were tired and eager to get into our warm house and snug into bed. When we got to the door Bill said, "I don't have the key. You'll have to use yours."

I reached into my purse, fumbled around—no key! "I don't have my key either," I said, worried, looking at Bill.

"Hmmm, I'll try the back door. Maybe we left it unlocked."

Bill went around the house and after some time, came back, "No luck. I tried the kitchen window and the back bedroom windows, they're tight as a drum."

He tried the front windows—locked tight.

I was concerned for Mother. Sitting in the cold car, she could take a cold or even pneumonia. I offered to start the motor and turn the heater on, but she would have none of it. I guess she was afraid of asphyxiation. Or did she simply not want to waste gasoline? I don't know. But she was adamant that the car motor should not be running.

Then Bill noticed, although it was midnight the neighbor's light was on. "I'm going to the Browns and see if I can borrow a ladder. Maybe I can get into the attic window."

I don't know why I didn't crawl into the car with Mother to get out of the damp cold. But, stunned, I just stood by the front door praying. Of course, I was praying! I'm always praying! Soon Bill and Mr. Brown came, each on an end of a long ladder. They put it up to the attic window. Bill climbed up, shook and jarred mightily on the window. "Paint-sealed tight!" he said as he backed down.

With a question mark on his face Bill said, "Maybe we'll have to drive to town and get a motel."

Just then a warm breeze gently brushed my right cheek and just as gently the door slowly moved wide open!

I can feel the warm breeze yet as it lightly brushed my cheek. I will always remember that wonderful gift from God—the Breath of His Spirit.

## JEWEL II
## A TAP ON THE SHOULDER

My second unforgettable miracle happened when my friend Ardith and I were working as surgical nurses in the hospital at Lebanon, Oregon. We heard about a speaker from the Far East. He was acclaimed a healer.

"Let's go hear him!" I said to Ardith. I was curious about the Indian from afar. Also, I wondered just how a "Healer" went about healing. That was the work I was in.

Ardith was game for the adventure. So after work we drove a short distance to the small church building where the services were held. When we entered, we were surprised there were so few in the audience. We sat listening as the minister spoke about spiritual healing and the laying on of hands. Then my attention was diverted by a tap on my shoulder. I looked at Ardith sitting beside me and said, "What is it?"

"Nothing," she replied, obviously not distracted as I was.

Again the tap came on my shoulder.

Again I looked at Ardith and said, "What is it, Ardith? What do you want?"

Ardith whispered, "I didn't say anything. Why?"

"You tapped me on the shoulder."

"No, I didn't."

We continued our whispered conversation.

"Someone tapped me on the shoulder, wasn't it you?"

"No."

I looked around. There were still few in the audience. No one sat behind me. Then I realized the severe pain, which I had for months in that shoulder, was gone.

The pain had been so debilitating, I could hardly raise my arm, let alone lift the surgical equipment and what's more, the patients! I feared I'd have to give up the first love of my nursing career, the surgery room.

Awed, I heard very little of the message and less of what the healer said as he went from one to another. I walked out of that building on air. I was jubilant! Healed!

To this day, twenty-some years later, I have no pain in that shoulder!

This miracle I celebrate every time I realize, but for the grace of God, I could have been forced by a painful shoulder to leave my greatest love, the operating room.

Except for the emergency room, all other hospital departments were too slow for me. I thrive on what others might see as stressful responsibility. The operating room was my domain. I managed it, controlled it. I made preparation for the doctors, helped prepare the patient, helped with the incision, with the total operation. I handed the doctor his instruments and helped make the suture. I was at the immediate scene of the emergency, making a difference in the life of a patient. What could be more rewarding in a lifetime of work?

To change would be a great loss. The operating room, that was where I belonged. It was my first love. And God, in his gracious goodness, assured me of that love. I will be forever grateful.

# CHAPTER 5

# I Died to Live

*names changed*

I live with my sister, Phyllis. This particular evening we were watching TV. I started to have excruciating pains in my chest. I feared the worst and asked Phyllis to take me to emergency. We just got into the car when I gasped. My spirit rose out of my body. My sister started beating on my chest. Later she told me my head fell forward, cutting off my breath. She quickly lifted my head so I could breathe and angrily pounded on my chest, yelling, "Damn you, Don, don't you die on me." When I started to breathe again, she rushed me to the hospital. The doctors examined me immediately and said I had a near fatal heart attack. It was Phyllis' beating on my chest that saved my life.

What she didn't know at the time was that I was not in the corpse she was beating on. I was above it. I saw her pounding on its chest.

When I rose out of my body I experienced total void. The horror of blackness was beyond description. Astronauts spoke of the "beautiful darkness" behind the moon. Let me tell you, there was nothing beautiful in this darkness. It was the deep, dark, terror and horror-filled blackness of hell, shut off from every vestige of good, of God, of warmth and light. I knew I was bound for that separation from God and all eternal goodness unless I changed my way of life.

Oh, I was having a good time in my old life. I owned restaurants and night clubs, traveled around the world, stayed in the most posh hotels and partied in elegant resorts and associated with influential people. "Wine, women and song," that was my self-consumed, guiding principle. I thought I was living the good life. I didn't even toss a scrap of thought toward God. I wasn't even sure I believed in him. I was far from being interested in trying the religious pursuit.

Down under all the surface pleasures, I knew I wasn't happy. But I was too busy flying around after my sensual pleasures to give it a thought. Fulfilling my ego-wants was uppermost in my mind. I had no interest in giving my soul thought or time. But the chilling experience of being cut off from every aspect of good, of all love, light, peace, joy, this was enough to wake me up.

When I recovered from my heart attack enough to recall the freezing cold of outer hell, I knew that my desires had changed. Hell was real and I didn't intend to go there. Heaven took on new interest for me and I have been pursuing the spiritual life ever since. The old haunts and pleasures are as empty as the blackness I experienced when I left my body and tasted the absolute despair of hell.

Now the depth of peace and joy I have as I walk with God are indescribably pleasurable.

# CHAPTER 6

# "Chief," Seminole Indian Boy

## *Freda Hamilton*

It was back in 1950, when my husband Bob and I were first married. We were sitting on a park bench in Shawnee, Oklahoma. A young boy came walking by. Bob was a school teacher and knew the boy. He called him by name, "Chief," (the only name we ever knew) and spoke to him. During the brief conversation, Bob asked Chief if he would go to Sunday School with us if we came and picked him up. Chief said yes, and gave Bob directions to his house: "One mile west of the cemetery on the northwest corner of the two section-line roads that crossed."

A few weeks later while driving Chief home, Bob asked if he knew other kids who might like to come to Sunday School. Chief said he had cousins who lived four miles up the unpaved road from him.

Chief's mother gave permission for Chief to go with Bob to the home of his cousins. This Coker family had nine children. When Bob approached their parents about the possibility of taking the children to Sunday School, the grandparents, who lived in an adjacent house, were consulted. After minutes of discussion in the Indian language, it was decided the children could go with us.

This launched our "ministry" of bringing children, youth and senior citizens to Sunday school and church.

Two years later we moved to Portland, Oregon. It was not difficult here to find someone to join us on our way to church. Our lives were greatly enriched by the wonderful friends we made. There was five-year-old "Gene-y" who brought his offering in a "lemelope," a girl who shared our son's birthday and one family who was quite special to us because they rode with us for eight years until the older girl had a driver's license and they no longer needed us to take them.

At one time, when I was cooking dinner, I felt a strong "urge" to go into the bedroom and pray. I had no idea what I was to pray about and anyway, I was busy cooking. Soon the urge became so strong I turned off all the burners, went into the bedroom, got on my knees and said, "Lord, here I am." I didn't know what else to do.

Then, as clear as anything, the words came to me, "You and Bob are going to win many souls for me."

I was shocked. We never thought we were doing much of anything. We did hope it would make a difference in some lives, but that would be very few. I wanted to ask some questions like, "How?" "When?" "What do you want us to do?" But the message was finished. I went back to cooking dinner.

Until now, I never told anyone this experience. It has been one of those "sacred moments." I felt no one else would understand.

Six or eight years passed. We were no longer transporting children. But we were working in various areas of the Sunday school.

Then—Bob was diagnosed with leukemia and became critically ill. I kept thinking of what God had spoken to me and I felt it had not been fulfilled. We planned to go on some short-term mission trips after we retired. So I kept holding onto the idea that the Lord had something more for us to do. Surely Bob would be restored to health, I thought. It was not so. As the years passed I considered some of those whose lives we had touched. For thirty years I had no direct contact with the two girls and the boy who had been so special to us for eight years.

In December of 2001 a lady handed me a check to pay for a Christmas tree on a lot where we were selling trees for a charity. When I saw the name on the check I said, "I hope you don't mind my asking, but I knew a family with this name. Do you know a Diane, Linda or Bobby?"

"Oh, yes," she said, "I'm married to their father. The girls are wonderful Christian women. And Robert is married. He and his wife attend church regularly."

In time I met the father too and learned he is now a Christian.

That scene lingered joyfully in my heart for days. I still get teary eyed when I think of it and of how good God has been to answer our prayers. Although our efforts were so small, our miracle-working God multiplied them and brought a whole family into his kingdom. And who knows what wonders may have happened in Chief's life and family. I know I'm going to be looking for "Cokers" when I get to heaven. I hope I see one named "Chief."

I think I will.

# CHAPTER 7

# A Walk on the Beach

## *Anita Merrill*

Years ago Adele taught me a special way to meditate and to feel close to Jesus. She told me to use my imagination. This instruction she received from Dr. E. Stanley Jones, in his book *Abundant Living*.

"We imagine everything else," she said. "We do everything first with our imaginations. Subconsciously we even imagine where the chair is under us, before we sit down. Haven't you ever thought the chair was in one place and it wasn't? Maybe someone pulled it out from under you and you fell down. But you imagined it was there.

"You imagine where a person is and direct your voice that way when you want to call or talk to them. Before you start to walk to someone you think and quickly imagine where they are. So much of this is subconscious.

"Just so, envision in your mind that you are walking up to Jesus. Then tell him what you need," she told me.

"Using your imagination, see him in a certain place, go up to him and just talk to him like you would to anyone else. The Bible says, 'God is spirit and they that worship him must worship him in spirit and in truth.' So this is a spiritual thing you do."

Now for many years I have imagined seeing Jesus physically when I want to talk to him. Here is one of those experiences.

I've had migraines for years. I used to get these very painful headaches that almost debilitated me. Often my vision was distorted so that I'd see only parts of an object and I'd see jagged lines, lines like an artist makes when he draws lightning. Or jagged plaids would be jumping before my eyes, even when I closed them. For instance, one time when I was driving the car, I saw a bicycle rider on the road. He had only a head and feet. He was pedaling with no body.

Too, I can't talk normally when I have a migraine. Words may come out garbled if I can say words at all. It's been diagnosed as "migraine-type episode." They usually last two or three days. For many years I didn't know about the medication I could take for it and I just suffered them out. They were almost totally debilitating and horrible. Severely sick, vomiting, with bad headaches, I felt they were driving me crazy.

One time when I had an episode, I couldn't stay awake. I was driving with my young daughter Kim in the car. I kept falling asleep. I told Kim I needed to pull over to the side of the road and nap a little before we could go on. Which I did. Fortunately, I could trust Kim to sit quietly and wait for me. If I had one of the boys I'd have had to go home.

In the doctor's office I fell asleep before it was my turn to see him. I just couldn't stay awake.

But for a few years now I've taken medication. I put the pill under my tongue and in a short while the headache goes away. But then I feel real yucky the rest of the day and maybe even the next. I hate to feel that way, but at least I can function. This time I had had the migraine for five days. I had so much to do, I didn't want to take the pill and feel real bad. But it was growing worse and worse.

On one of these days, a man called me about a matter I was working on. My husband, Del answered the phone and handed it to me. I couldn't talk. Finally, with garbled words that sounded like pigeon English, I got the message out that I had a severe headache and couldn't talk. It was very embarrassing.

A similar thing happened at the post office. I needed to send a check and wanted a receipt to show the date I sent it. I struggled to talk, but couldn't say anything.

The woman said, "Are you having a lapse?"

I wanted to say, "a migraine," but the best I could do was say "headache."

"Is it migraine?" she asked.

I nodded, "Yes."

She took care of my need and I drove home.

Del suggested I lie down and relax, maybe that would ease it. I did and while I was lying in bed I thought, I'm going to meditate the way Adele taught me.

I envisioned myself walking on the beach. Jesus was sitting on a rock a distance away. I saw myself walking slowly toward him. When I got there I just knelt before him and said, "Oh, God, there is something wrong in my head. Please make it go away. Take away the flashing. Just heal me."

Jesus didn't say a word. He laid his hand on my head and the jagged flashing stopped and my head quit hurting.

It seemed too fast. It was unbelievable to me that it would happen so fast. I waited to see if it was really gone. I didn't feel sick anymore. It didn't seem possible that it would really be gone. So I just lay there waiting to see if it was real—to see if it would flash again. But it didn't. Then I got up and went back to work. The migraine was gone.

Of course, you know I was very grateful.

# CHAPTER 8

# My Seven-Month Journey with Cancer

*Jan Linamen*

In January, 2003 a persistent cough and hardness in my abdomen sent me to the doctor. Immediately Dr. Bill Anderson scheduled me for blood tests and ultrasound—tests at the hospital and on Sunday.

In a couple days the doctor called us to his office. With compassion, he told my husband, Harold, and me that I had cancer in the lungs, liver, kidneys and spleen—four places! Lymphoma was at stage 4. (Stage 5 is death.)

We were numb. I had cancer!

No, we had cancer—the spouse, too, suffers everything. We felt helpless, totally out of control. Our only comfort was our faith that God was in control of our lives. That brought a measure of peace.

Dr. Anderson made an appointment for me with an oncologist here in our home town of Anderson, Indiana. The appointment was two weeks away. Then we received a call saying our appointment was set back another two weeks, or we could chose a different oncologist.

The wait seemed too long.

My nephew's wife, Dr. Agnes J. Schrader, is a nephrologist (kidney specialist). She recommended her friend, a hematologist/oncologist (blood/cancer specialist), Dr. Rumen E. Birhiray. She contacted him that night. He agreed to see me the next morning on January 16. My chemo treatments started the 17th.

Dr. Birhiray is Nigerian-American. He earned his M.D. from the University of Benin, Nigeria and completed fellowships in bone marrow transplant and medical oncology at Johns Hopkins University and The National Cancer Institute in Bethesda, Maryland.

We were pleased to learn Dr. Birhiray was a Christian. He is very gentle and compassionate. One day, after giving me some bad news, he hugged me and told me he would be praying for me over the weekend. This strengthened our confidence that God was in this with us.

I was concerned about my hospital history. It was poor. At two hospitals the nurses asked me not to come back unless I was a patient. At one, I visited my mother who had breast surgery. I walked to her bed and fainted. Out cold, I fell right on top of her. When I came to I was sitting on a chair in the doorway with my head between my knees. One nurse was holding me, another held smelling salts to my nose.

"Please don't come back," the nurse holding me said, "we're too busy to care for both you and your mother."

Years later, at the second hospital, the nurse invited me to stay away. I fainted while visiting my father in ICU. This time I was put on a gurney and my younger brother wheeled me into the emergency room. He checked me in by my maiden name. The attending nurse insisted on testing me before she'd release me. She asked me my name. I gave her my married name.

"Nope," she said "that is not your name."

"Then who am I?" I asked.

She questioned me further. I told her the name she had was my maiden name. Finally she believed I was mentally stable, did know who I was, and released me.

"Please," she said firmly, "don't come back unless you're sick and need medical attention."

It's so embarrassing! I've passed out when seeing blood drawn, my own or another's, and even when visiting a very ill friend. Now, how would I deal with all the cancer treatment processes? This was a serious concern.

Too, our family has a history of cancer. Three aunts and two cousins died of cancer. At the time of this writing, two more cousins suffer from cancer. Was it now my turn to die of this dreaded disease? Fear haunted me.

In the night when everything was still—my husband Harold and our dog Shadow both asleep, a sinister voice spoke hauntingly in my brain.

"You have cancer! You are going to die!"

To drown out the voice I quoted hymns: "Blessed Assurance Jesus Is Mine," "Great Is Thy Faithfulness," "Jesus Loves Me, this I Know." These were my comfort.

Another strategy I devised was to flood my mind with peaceful sights and sounds.

When growing up, I lived on Tappan Lake in Michigan. A road went through the lake. Often we took this road to get to our house. Many times on my way home, I stopped the car close to the water's edge. Here I sat, quietly watching the sun as it sparkled on the ripples. I'd listen to the sound of the waves as they lapped the shore. In long, peaceful moments I'd let my mind roam. Often I imagined Jesus standing in a boat, coming toward me with His hands outstretched. He was reaching for me—no one else but me.

"Jesus, Jesus, Jesus!" I cried.

Over and over again I envisioned this scene. Sitting in the quiet of the night, I'd let the sound of the water wash over me. I'd see Jesus come to me. Comfort came with the feeling we were together, just Jesus and me. I surrendered myself and my future into Jesus' hands.

Six chemo treatments, 30 bags of fluid in my veins, many CT scans, PET Scan, Ultrasounds, biopsies, blood drawn again and again, shots given, test for blood clots, tests on heart (to see if chemo damaged it). Needles, needles, needles and miraculously, I did not faint once!

Side effects from chemotherapy were weakness and complete exhaustion. In killing the cancer cells, good cells were killed too. I was—
too weak to hold my head up,
too weak to hold a book—Harold read to me,
hair on my head, eyebrows, eyelashes all gone,
fingernails peeled off—big toenails, too,
mouth, tongue, corners of mouth all covered with sores,
eating—painful, very difficult,
too weak to walk,
had to walk anyway—to keep from getting blood clots—held onto table and kept putting one foot in front of the other,
stooped down to pick up something—couldn't get back up alone.

It was a long, hard, grueling battle. I felt an identity with Jesus' agony in the Garden of Gethsemane. I tasted of His death and burial.

The words of this song tell my story as well as Jesus'.

Have you had a Gethsemane?
In the garden He went to pray
When it seemed hope was gone
He prayed with a broken heart
And He prayed all alone

Have you had a Gethsemane?
Have you prayed in despair?
In the dark of those weary hours
Did the Lord meet you there?

Have you had a Gethsemane?
Have you prayed the night through?
Have you shed tears of agony
When no hope was in view?
Have you prayed, "If it be Thy will
May this cup pass from me"?

But if it's thy will, dear Lord
I will bear it for thee.

Have you had a Gethsemane?

Have you had a Gethsemane? I have!

## MY GETHSEMANE

As Jesus prayed in the Garden of Gethsemane, "Let this cup pass from me," so I prayed, "Lord, don't let this happen to me."

There were many reasons why I should not die. I made a list.

I don't want Harold to go through this again. (His first wife died of cancer.)

I don't want to die before my mother. The child shouldn't go first.

I have unfinished ironing to do.

I need to clean the garage.

I need to reorganize the attic.

I need to plant flowers in the spring.

I plan to mow our lawn this spring and summer.

Cancer does NOT fit into my schedule.

But cancer didn't concern itself with my schedule.

## MY DEATH AND (FIRST) BURIAL

When Jesus died, he was placed in a tomb—then a stone was rolled against the entrance. I had to "die" to all those I loved and to all my personal possessions. Again I made a list.

My piano and keyboard—

I want someone to play these instruments and fill their heart and home with beautiful music.

My CD's, tapes and LP's (300 LP's)—

I want someone to play these on a stereo—sing and worship while they listen.

My collection of bone china cups and saucers—

I want people to sit around their table, drinking tea and eating cookies while sharing the concerns and thanks givings on their hearts, as we did many times around our table.

My sewing machine—

At one time it made all of my children's clothes and mine. I had much pleasure in designing outfits, purchasing fabric and making garments. I want someone to sew as I have and enjoy the satisfaction of finished garments.

My books—

I can see someone cuddled up on a sofa, reading and enjoying my books. I hope they'll take good care of them as I do.

My friends—

I have to say goodbye to my dear husband, my family and friends. How do you say goodbye to all those you have loved and enjoyed so much, friendships developed over a life-time, some college roommates from way back in the 1950's?

Although I struggled hard against it, all these treasures, and many more I gave up. I surrendered them, buried them, and rolled a stone onto the grave.

I did that! I really did!

## MY FUNERAL

Jesus prayed in the Garden of Gethsemane, died and was buried. Now that was my lot. I planned my funeral. Not much needed to be said. I have no credentials, no great accomplishment, done nothing of importance. No speaker would be needed.

"Since I love music and people most of all, just make my funeral service a singspiration," I suggested. "Make it a happy occasion. Let them know I plan to be a soloist when I get to heaven. I'll wear a long, light blue gown. The angels will be my backup. Harps my accompaniment. It will be wonderful!"

Then came—

MY RESURRECTION

Oh, glorious resurrection!

On July 25, 2003 Dr. Birhiray announced to us, "Your cancer is in remission."

REMISSION!

OH, THE CELEBRATION!

Tears of joy,

Long, warm hugs,

Loud laughs,

Shouts of praise.

Joyous thanks

to our Lord,

to our doctors,

Heart-praise beyond words,

Happy calls,

to family,

to friends,

More tears of joy,

More hugs and laughter!

Shouts—I'm alive! I'm alive!

After Jesus was in the tomb for three days, he rose from the grave. The resurrection brought new life. This is what happened to me.

MY NEW LIFE

There are no words equal to this occasion, none which adequately express my joy in living. No words sufficient to give praise to God for his gifts of life and love. No words can fully express my thankfulness to Jesus for his constant presence and the faith given to trust that HE WAS IN CONTROL.

My gratitude is inexpressible to—

My dear Harold, tender and loving care giver, efficient housekeeper, compassionate and patient encourager,

Many who gave loving help, food, care and prayer: our church family at Park Place Church of God in Anderson, Indiana, especially the Pathways Class,

People from places around the world—Lebanon, Japan, and Barbados to name a few—encouraging calls, mail, email,
All who sent cards, notes, flowers in abundance,
Greatest of all, Lord Jesus, who manifested love in so many ways—
To Him we pour out our hearts of overflowing gratitude.

## PROCLAMATION AND RETROSPECTION

I wish I could tell the world how I, too, experienced the Bible verse of Mtt. 14:35 NIV. "People brought all their sick to Him (Jesus) and begged Him to let the sick just touch the edge of his cloak, and all who touched him were healed."

Jesus healed me!

I could feel Jesus' presence with me all the painful, fearful, agonizing! seven months.

He was my closest friend.

I asked Him to wrap His arms around me, to hold me when I was afraid and didn't know what to expect.

I knew He understood my feelings and my fears.

Many times I just said His name and felt He heard my heart's cry.

Many nights I didn't know how to pray. I lay in bed and repeated His name "Jesus," "Jesus," over and over and over again until dawn broke.

I could feel that He heard me.

How true the words of this Gaither song—

Jesus, Jesus, Jesus
There's just something about that name.

For me, there will always be, throughout time and eternity, something about that glorious name, "Jesus."

# CHAPTER 9

# Flying with Angels

## *Karen Anliker*

Christmas of 1964 I was fourteen years old, and lived in the small town of Rhododendron, Oregon, located on the foothills of Mt. Hood. The winter season had already brought heavy snowfall. Eighteen inches covered the ground. Then over night a Chinook wind blew in with heavy rain. Quickly the snow melted. The frozen ground could not absorb the water. The rivers rose with angry torrents.

Our home was situated between Zig Zag River and Still Creek. We could hear the roar of large boulders as they rolled with force in the ever-increasing torrent. Because of the weather conditions, we did not have running water that morning and my Mom decided to keep my brothers and me home from school. Then my Dad and brothers went up town to see what was going on and to check out the conditions of the river at other vantage points. Mom and I decided to walk the quarter mile to the bridge that crossed over the Zig Zag. As we stood on our side of the bridge, we were in awe of the strength and magnitude of the high water. The river had already risen to touch the under side of the bridge.

While standing there, a car coming from the other side stopped before crossing. Two young teen age boys jumped out and ran across the bridge to where we were. While they stood talking to my Mom, I noticed other boys I knew standing at the other end of the bridge. Without waiting for Mom to say yes or no, I darted out to talk to them. If the bridge is safe enough for the boys to come, it's safe enough for me to go, I thought.

Just then I felt the bridge move as it broke away from the other side. Thoughtlessly, I continued to run and jump. Somehow, I landed safely on the other side. I watched the bridge as it washed down the raging river.

Later, as I pondered the experience, I remembered the hands underneath my arms as I flew across the raging span. My angels were there lifting and flying me to safety.

# CHAPTER 10

# Healing Back Pain

## *Denton Fair*

Trying to start my lawn mower, I pulled the cord twice. The third time it backfired with force that threw me to the ground. Violent pain shot through my body—so severe I couldn't get up. I called my wife, Aline. Sweat and tears ran down my face as we struggled to get me into the house, then into the car and into the doctor's office.

After examination and x-rays, Dr. Dandridge, an orthopedic surgeon, told me I had a slipped disk. He gave me strong pain medicine and muscle relaxers and sent me home to bed. He said if the relaxers didn't help the disk to heal I'd have to have surgery to fuse the vertebrae together so they would not press on the sciatic nerve.

For ten days I lay in bed taking the medication. Even so the pain was nearly unbearable. I couldn't sit up or walk to the bathroom without Aline's help and with dreadful pain. She coaxed me to try to sit at the table to eat but the pain was so severe I had no appetite. The only way I could be out of bed was to sit in the living room on our big, soft, Boston rocker.

There I could recline and at least be out of bed, but still not out of brutal pain.

The second Sunday of my confinement Aline asked if I would be all right if she left me to go to church to teach her Sunday school class. Her assistant was away and Aline felt she should be there. I agreed, and she helped me into the Boston rocker and turned the TV on to a channel with religious programs. This way I could watch church services while she was gone.

Shortly after Aline left home a program came on from a big church in Ohio. The announcer said Spanky McFarland was there that day and he would participate in the service. He said Spanky, unable to walk, had been incapacitated and confined to a wheel chair for many years.

I loved Spanky McFarland from the time I was a seven-year-old youngster. He was the leader of "Our Gang" comedies that came on TV every Saturday morning. I was always glued to the screen as these six kids pulled off their hilarious antics. Alfalfa was a little black kid with his front teeth out. He was my next favorite. Sparky, another member, had a twig of hair that stood straight up in front of his head. I don't remember the names of the other three. They were all funny, but my favorite was freckled-faced, pudgy-cheeked Spanky. He had energy and ingenuity, always leading the pack into startling and riotous mischief. I could identify with him.

Now, I was prejudiced against women preachers. Of all of them, I liked gangly, un-beautiful, dramatic and slurred-talking Katheryn Koehlman the very least. In fact, I rebelled against her so strongly I almost—well, let's just say I resented her. At any other time I wouldn't sit for two hours and listen to her. But three things kept me from turning the nob of my 1950's vintage TV to a different channel. One, I couldn't get up off the chair and walk to the TV without overwhelming pain. Two, after all those years, I wanted to see Spanky again in his grown-up form. And three, I was curious to see what Katheryn Koehlman would do with Spanky.

I was a Christian, but a sceptical one.

At one point Miss Koehlman called Spanky onto the stage. Two big men lifted him up in his wheel chair. There he sat before my eyes, Spanky

McFarland, my favorite kid actor! I really did love him. Right then I felt the rush of excitement and love that I had for him when I was a kid. It flooded back over me. I couldn't believe I was actually seeing my old pal, Spanky, again.

Katheryn focused those sharp, brown eyes directly on Spanky. With her distinct, drawn-out and full-tongued speech she said, "Spanky McFarland, God is going to heal you tonight! I am going to anoint you with oil and pray for you and God is going to heal you!"

At that my prejudice dropped off. My faith stirred. I didn't care what Katheryn Koehlman looked or sounded like, I just wanted to see Spanky McFarland, my old buddy, get healed. I grew anxious, eager for this miracle to really happen.

Katheryn Koehlman was so positive saying, "Spanky McFarland, you are going to be healed today! God is going to heal you and enable you to walk."

At that I felt my faith rise, so badly I wanted healing for my friend.

Miss Koehlman's long, bony fingers touched Spanky's forehead with the anointing oil. Then she laid her hand on his head and said a slurred prayer. Then, looking into Spanky's eyes, she said, "You are healed! You can walk now! Come out of that wheel chair in the name of Jesus and walk!"

Spanky wriggled forward in the chair, put his feet under him, pulled himself forward by the arm rests and rose to his feet. The audience went wild with clapping and cheers as Spanky, in his braces, hobbled forward toward Katheryn.

She said, "Go to the men's room, down the hall and around the corner, and take off those braces. You don't need them anymore. And come walking out here."

When Spanky came back walking strong and firm the audience went wild again, clapping, whistling, and shouting praises to God.

Katheryn Koehlman turned around and looking straight into the TV camera said, "There are people out there in the viewing audience with back pain who are watching this. They too can be healed today."

Then she turned 180 degrees and pointed right at me where I was sitting in my Boston rocker. Looking sharply at me, she said, "God is going to heal you, too! What happened to Spanky is going to happen to you!"

Faith welled up inside me and washed all over me. I knew she was talking specifically to me.

I believed.

When Aline came home I was still sitting in my rocker. I said, "I've been healed. I know I can get up now and walk."

While I was still sitting there, relating this experience to Aline, my good friend Jim Gaily came in to check on me because I missed church. When I related my experience to him, he wept and threw himself on me with tearful and joyful hugs. He straightened himself up and said, with quivering breath, "Brother, I want to wash your feet." (a religious act of servitude)

Aline got a pan of water. And right there, in my house, with me still sitting in the rocker, Jim knelt down and gently poured the warm water over my feet. He dried them with the towel Aline brought. I stood up. Jim and I fell into each other's arms, both weeping for the great joy of God's miraculous goodness. We hugged, laughed and with tears streaming down both our faces, praised God together.

There I stood, completely free of pain.

That night, for the first time in ten days, I slept in my bed, soundly. I rose up the next morning, showered, dressed, had a hearty breakfast and went to work.

In the following forty-three years I have worked, lifted, gardened and done anything I've wanted to do and have not had one day of back pain.

Here I had a miracle that gave me freedom to live, work and praise God. And that I do right heartily! Oh, yes, I'm learning not to criticize God's servants. Regardless of our prejudices, God will use whomever he chooses.

# CHAPTER 11

# Tessa's Leap for Life

## *Ginger Dixon*

Of miracles I have many. But let me tell you my favorite multi-miracled story. I have this darling horse. Her name is Tessa. I bought her when she was eight years old. As of this writing she is thirty-one. That's pretty old for a horse.

I didn't know horses lived to be that old. But she has.

Tessa's a little stiffy. But she gets along fine. She gets her daily vitamins and MSM and we take rides together in the berry fields of Gresham, Oregon—not big, long rides like we used to, just short ones, a half-hour or so.

Years earlier, down in the San Davonia Mountains, near Los Angeles, my then-husband Bob and I went for a ride in the Willamette Forest. He had a horse about the same size as mine. Tessa is short, 14/2 (hands). That's about five-foot at the shoulder, which means she's barely over my shoulders. She's palomino: blond with flaxen main and tail. She has a bit of Arab in her which gives her self-pride. She's cute and pretty and has she got personality! Tessa has been the joy of my life. She's the one being I will take out alone and share times with God.

Often times when I was troubled, she and I went out into the mountains and the shrub brush together, getting away from it all.

Well, this particular day we rode in the mountains with my then-husband Bob and his horse. Bob saw a sign that said, "Rosey's Grave." Sometimes these signs just mark a path. He started riding his horse down this foot path. I told him it wasn't safe. But he wouldn't believe me.

Do you have those times when you instinctively know something? This was one of them. I could feel that the path was not safe.

Bob went on to take the horses down this foot path. Horses get what they call barn soror. "Soror" is French for sister. Sorority comes from that. Horses get attached to each other and one will not leave the other. Bob's horse was the aggressive type. She always wanted to see what was over the next hill—and the next and the next. She should have been an endurance-riding horse.

Down the path we went until we came to a stream. It was on a forty-five degree downward angle. I knew it was dangerous and I told Bob so. He didn't listen, just rode his horse into the stream.

"It's dangerous and I'm not crossing this river!" I shouted.

But Bob kept going. He wanted to find what he was after: "Rosey's Grave."

"It's right here!" I shouted, "It's this path!"

But he wouldn't believe me. He rode across.

I had this strong foreboding. "It's not safe! It's dangerous!" that "Something" inside of me said.

I prayed.

Literally, I crossed my fingers and said, "Please, God, protect us."

I thought we'd be okay.

Unknown to me, Bob's horse broke up the shale on the bottom of the river.

When Tessa and I got to the middle of the river, the broken shale started drifting. Tessa's feet went out from under her. As she flipped over this "Something" told me to pull my leg up. I did and Tessa landed beside me. Had she landed on me, my leg would have been broken. Also, this

"Something" told me instantly to keep Tessa's legs straight, which guarded them from getting broken as we drifted down steam.

Bob was up on a ten-foot bank. "Throw me the lead rope," he shouted.

I did. And he caught it.

"Come Tessa," He called.

I was screaming angry words at him even as I was sighing for "Unseen Help." Then all of a sudden, Tessa stood straight up, leaped over my head and flew up the ten foot bank and landed upright on the path directly behind Bob's horse.

I pulled myself out of the river and up the bank by the lead rope. While standing by Bob, still shouting my anger at him for putting us in such a hazardous way, he said, "Now look behind you."

I looked back at the river just as the shale we were on pitched over the edge of the water fall. In minutes we would have plunged to our death, both mine and my precious little friend, Tessa's.

Later we learned that cliff had a thirty-foot drop.

We had multiplied miracles. No one could gainsay that.

1. Tessa did not fall on my leg to break it.

2. I straightened Tessa's legs out so they were not broken while we drifted down the river.

3. We were not carried down stream another three feet and pitched over a thirty-foot waterfall.

4. Tessa could stand up in the moving stream and leap over my head. No way, of her own, could a little five-foot mare, standing still, leap over a person just as tall as she was.

5. Tessa leaped up a ten-foot bank. No way could a common little riding horse leap up a ten-foot bank. Not even a tall, trained horse could do that.

Angels or another "Unseen Force" picked this little mare up, carried her over my head and up a ten-foot bank and set her upright, square on the path next to her sister horse. That was more than just one miracle.

Here is the more:

1. I was told the path was not safe and therefore alert to danger.
2. I was told to save my leg from being broken under Tessa in her fall.
3. Tessa's legs did not get broken when she fell in the stream.
4. I was told to keep Tessa's legs straight as we were drifting down river.
5. Tessa was able to stand up on her own as we were moving in the current.
6. We were able to negotiate these many maneuvers before the shale we were on broke away and washed over the cliff.
7. I could throw a rope accurately enough the first time for Bob to catch it! That had to be a miracle!
8. I could shinny up a ten-foot bank with no help but a rope.
9. I had swiftness of thought and hand to do all the things I was told to do in so short a time.

*****

Miracles—multiplied by miracles!

Evidently God still had things for Tessa and me to do together. Now she's still giving me the warm, loving pleasure she's given me all these years.

My prayer of gratitude:

Thanks to You, God, and all Your ministering angels.

And thanks too for my beloved little friend, Tessa.

By the way, Bob never did find Rosey's Grave but he created a situation that almost called for two other graves, Tessa's and mine.

# CHAPTER 12

# Breath of God

*name withheld*

"Life's a little thing." Robert Browning once said that. But a little thing can also mean life. How well I remember. Two years ago in downtown Denver, my friend Scott and I saw something quite insignificant happen. But it changed the world for two people. However, neither one of them seemed to notice.

It happened on one of those beautiful Denver days—crystal clear, no humidity, not a cloud in the sky. Rather than take the shuttle bus that runs up and down the Sixteenth Street Mall, we decided to walk the ten blocks from our work to an outdoor restaurant. The restaurant, in the shape of a baseball diamond, was called The Blake Street Baseball Club. The tables were set appropriately on the grass infield. Many colorful pennants and flags hung limply overhead.

As we sat outside, the sun continued to beat down on us and it became increasingly hot. There wasn't a hint of breeze. Heat radiated up from the table top. Nothing moved, except the waiters. And they didn't move fast.

After lunch, Scott and I started to walk back up the mall. We both noticed a mother and her young daughter walking out of a card shop toward the street. The mother was holding her daughter by the hand while reading a greeting card. It was immediately apparent to us that she was so engrossed in the card that she did not notice the shuttle bus moving toward her at a good clip. She and her daughter were just one step from disaster. Scott started to yell. He hadn't got a word out of his mouth, when a breeze blew the card out of the mother's hand and over her shoulder. She spun around and grabbed at the card, nearly knocking her daughter down. By the time she picked the card up from the ground and turned back around to cross the street, the shuttle bus had whizzed by. She never knew what almost happened.

To this day two things continue to perplex me about the incident. First, where did that one spurt of wind come from to blow the card out of the young mother's hand? There had not been a whisper of wind at lunch or during our long walk back up the mall. Second, if Scott had been able to get his words out, the young mother might have looked up at us and continued to walk—right into the bus. It was the wind that made the difference. It blew the card from her hand so she had to step away from the bus to retrieve it. Stepping in that direction saved her life and the life of her daughter.

The passing bus did not create the wind. On the contrary, the wind came from the opposite direction. I have no doubt it was a breath from God protecting the mother and child. But the awesomeness of this miracle is that she never knew.

As we walked back to work, I wondered how often God acts in our lives without our awareness. Here the difference between life and death was a very little thing, just a breeze.

No doubt miracles often blow unseen through our lives.

# CHAPTER 13

# My Miracle

## *Bobby Naef*

On March 18, 2001, at the age of ten, I was baptized at our church. This is my testimony I gave to the congregation. Adele Hooker asked me to let her put it in her book because she knew I felt it was my personal miracle. I hope it helps some other kid to have a miracle, too.

*****

I first accepted Jesus into my heart when I was four years old. When I was real young, my mom taught my Sunday school class, partly because I would cry if she didn't stay in class with me. I still remember one of the Bible verses from my three-year-old class. We used to dance around the room as we sang, "Let us come near to God with a sincere heart. Hebrews ten twenty-two."

My parents got divorced about three years ago, which caused me to wonder if God was real. So I wrote this note to my mom that said: "God has never proved himself to me, so how do I know that he exists?"

After my mom read it, she suggested we pray and ask God to make himself real to me in some way. She said, "If we are truly seeking God, he will make himself known to us."

So we prayed and a lot of our prayers were answered. One of the bigger answers to prayer happened when I had to give a long speech for school. It was late at night and I was trying to memorize the speech for the next day. I couldn't seem to get it. I was frustrated and upset. Finally, my mom said that I should go to bed. We prayed together that God would use this opportunity to show how much he cared for me. We asked that he would put the speech clearly in my mind while I slept.

He did it!

The next morning I was able to say the speech perfectly without any more practice. God made himself real to me!

Since that letter I wrote to my mom and that experience as well as others, I truly feel the presence of God in my life! I prayed to God asking Jesus to be the savior of my life. Now I am here being baptized following God's word.

I believe.

# CHAPTER 14

# Mackenzie's Prayer

## *Aline Fair*

"Mommie, is Grandma Edwards dead?" Mackenzie, our four-and a-half-year-old great-granddaughter, asked her mother while the family of five were driving down highway 67 from Fort Wayne to Anderson, Indiana. They were on their way to visit Mackenzie's grandparents, Phil and Betty Fair, and us, her great-grandparents. My mother, Mary Edwards, is Mackenzie's great-great-grandmother. She was 105 1/2 years old at the time.

"No," said, Suze, "Grandma Edwards is not dead. Why did you ask?"

"I feel like Jesus wants me to pray that Grandma Edwards won't get dead," the little one said.

Kelly and Suze, Mackenzie's parents, are always pleased when their children want to pray, for whatever reason.

"Well, Honey," Suze said, "if you feel Jesus wants you to pray, you pray. We'll bow our heads and pray with you."

With that Mackenzie's brother Ben, sister Katie and mother Suze, bowed their heads. Daddy Kelly had to keep his eyes on the road but he prayed just as earnestly and with thanksgiving that his child had a tender heart toward Jesus.

I was told Mackenzie's words were sweet and filled with relaxed faith as she said, "Dear Lord Jesus, please help Great-Great-Grandma Edwards not to get dead. Thank you, amen."

Grandma Edwards, my mother, is reasonably well, partially blind, but keen of intellect. She lives by herself in an assisted living apartment at the Broadway Manor in Muskogee, Oklahoma. On Sundays she usually has dinner with my brother, Orville and his wife, Emily. This day she lay on the sofa to take a nap while dinner was being prepared. When Emily called, she didn't respond. Nor could she be aroused. At the 911 call the ambulance came and took her to the Muskogee Regional Center

Emily called me to tell us about Mother and asked that we pray for her. We prayed.

Emily called again to give us the good news. At the Center, Mother was diagnosed as having congestive heart failure. For four hours the medical staff could not bring her to consciousness. And then, all at once, she awakened and said, "Where am I? Have I been asleep?"

When Kelly and his family arrived in Anderson we learned of Mackenzie's prayer. We called Emily to tell her about it. Emily said that was precisely the time when Grandma Edwards awakened.

In a few days Mother was back in her apartment, living alone at the Manor.

I'm sure the touch from God on Mackenzie's tender life will not soon be forgotten. I can hear Jesus say again, "Of such is the Kingdom of Heaven."

Another thing will not soon be forgotten, that is the telephone call I received from Mother a year later, just before lunch today.

She said, "Honey, I had three prayer meetings already this morning. Three different ladies came and asked me for prayer."

"The first lady came months earlier," Mama said, "asking me to pray for her son. While on his job, he fell from a tall building. Both arms were broken and much of the rest of his body was crushed. He was not expected to live. If he did, the doctor said he'd be badly crippled."

Mama prayed with the young man's mother.

"Today," Mama said, "she came to tell me her son recovered totally. He is like brand new and back to work. She wanted to thank me for my prayers."

Together they had a prayer meeting of thanksgiving to God for the miracle of total healing.

The second prayer meeting was for guidance. One of the aides at the Manor came to Mama. "I need direction for my life," the aide said. "I just don't know what I want to do. I want you to pray with me that I will find direction for my life."

Mama and the girl had a prayer meeting. Mama asked God to put his hand on this child of His and guide her in the path He wanted her to go. She thanked Mama and went happily back to work.

Number three was about a long-time friend of ours and of Sam's and Adele's (the author). It was Mary Jane Pamplin. Sam performed her's and her husband Odell's wedding. Now they celebrated their fiftieth wedding anniversary.

Odell's boss gave them a Caribbean cruise for their anniversary gift. Mary Jane came to Mary Edwards for a prayer of thanksgiving and also to pray for their safety.

"We've never been on a ship before," Mary Jane said. "We're nervous. Pray that we'll have a safe and a good trip."

And so Mama had three prayer meetings before the noon hour and she had to tell someone. She called in an excited voice.

Mama is 106 1/2 now and her mind is bright as a dollar. I chided her a bit.

"And just yesterday you said you didn't know why God left you here so long. Now I guess He told you why."

"Well," she said sheepishly, "I guess His children still need me. I do feel like a mother to them all."

But for Mackenzie's prayer, Great-Great-Grandma Edwards may not have been here to enjoy these helpful, pleasant and rewarding, morning prayer meetings.

# CHAPTER 15

# Surrender

## *Denton Fair*

In 1970 I was active in our local church in Muskogee, Oklahoma. I was in leadership. In fact, I was pastoring a small flock of people who were planting a new church. Here I preached in the morning service and in the evening meeting laymen spoke or preached.

For several months we met in homes or in an elementary school auditorium. Then we found a Methodist church which had dwindled down to where the District Superintendent offered to sell it to us at a reasonable price. We secured the property and became the Eastside Church of God. All this while I was working for the Corning Glass Works as the company controller.

One day a group of our church members drove the 100 miles to Oklahoma City where the Westridge Hills Church of God was having a Christian Brotherhood Hour Rally. Dr. Sterner from Anderson, Indiana, (our church headquarters) was then chairman and speaker of CBH, our denomination's international radio program. He was now the speaker of this rally in OK. City. The church was full to overflowing. Folding chairs were brought in to accommodate the large group. Everything was just great except that I had a headache that almost drove me crazy. For six weeks my head nearly burst. Our physician, Dr. Reynolds, couldn't figure out what was wrong nor how to help alleviate my pain. He gave me the strongest pain medicines. They didn't faze it. Even "Dylanton," normally given for seizures, didn't relieve the pain.

But I loved to hear Dr. Sterner preach and this was an unusual opportunity. Sitting, with our little group toward the front of the auditorium, I just toughed it out.

Our son, Phil, was the worship leader that evening. And who should he call on to lead in prayer?—Me!

I was just a layman. There were seven ministers in the congregation. I questioned to myself, Why is Phil asking me to pray when there are all these preachers here? He's never asked me to pray in a service before. Feeling inadequate in front of the large, preacher-packed sanctuary and with a splitting headache, I rose and did my best.

When Dr. Sterner got up to preach he walked slowly to the lectern. He said, "Tonight I'm going to speak on 'How God can make you a whole man: physically, mentally and spiritually.'"

He just waged into his message without introduction or warm up. It was powerful and without let up. In spite of my pounding head, I was fully alert and intimately involved in all Reverend Sterner said. In fact, I felt his whole message was directed precisely toward me. I thought, He doesn't know me. Why is he directing his whole message right at me. He's even pointing his finger at me. I knew what Sterner was preaching about was what I needed. I needed to be a "whole man." I wasn't as committed spiritually as I should be. I knew I needed to make a deeper surrender. I needed to be filled with the Holy Spirit. And I sure needed a physical healing for that abominable pain in my head. But I was a leading layman, and I was pretty well known in the state.

What would all these people think of me if I went to the altar? They'd think, "Wonder what's wrong with Denton?"

A swirl of thoughts was going around in my head. Just that morning I had been to a funeral of a person who had recently been converted. I admired his humility. He'd do anything in the church: mow lawns, wash windows, even clean toilets. Tony Chase was a Cherokee Indian. I stood at his coffin and looked at him admiringly. Then I prayed silently, "Lord, would you lay Tony's spirit of humility on me?"

Now, I realized I was standing here in the church rebelling and arguing with the Lord over going to the altar. In my ear I heard the Lord say, "I thought you asked me for Tony's spirit of humility." Then I heard these searing words which I will never forget. God said in strong, emphatic tone, "This is your last chance, Big Boy!"

With that I shot out of the pew like a bullet from a pistol and headed straight for the altar. I knelt in humility. Several ministers came to lay hands on me and pray. One asked, "What can we pray with you for, Brother?"

Humbly I answered, "I want to be the whole man that Brother Sterner preached about. I want to be cleansed and filled with the Holy Spirit and be delivered of this headache which I've had, day and night, for eight weeks."

Too, I was stressed over the fact that I was due to go to Corning's head office in New York. I was fearful of flying. Every other time I went on the train. Frankly, I was afraid the plane would go down and I wasn't sure where I'd go after the deadly crash. I wasn't certain I'd get into heaven.

There at the altar I told God I'd do anything he wanted me to do. I'd go any where he wanted me to go. It was a solemn commitment from the depths of my heart. I meant it for good and forever.

One of the preachers prayed for me and there was a rousing "Amen" from the others.

Right then the dark cloud of fear lifted off my whole being. I was set free! I felt free as a bird! However, my headache didn't go away.

It was on the way home, about half way between Muskogee and Oklahoma City, that all of a sudden, I realized my head didn't ache. I exclaimed, "Shorty, (my nickname for Aline) my headache's gone! I feel so free. I don't have any more fear at all. I can get on that plane and if it goes down, I know where I'm going!" No more would I ride the clanking and stopping-at-every-small-town train where I couldn't sleep all night. Six times I traveled that way. Now that was over!

However, a new set of circumstances appeared on the screen. These would severely challenge the commitment I made to God at the altar that night.

After only twelve months I received a telephone call from Dr. Lester Crose who was head of our denomination's missionary board. He wanted to come to Muskogee from Anderson to interview me for the position of controller. He said Dr. Sterner said for him to call me because the missionary board was in financial trouble and he felt I could do something about it. Dr. Crose came. He described the job of controller and the church's missions program. He told me of the salary. It was half of what I earned at Corning and with no other benefits. But they would move me and my wife to Anderson. They would give me a month's expenses to go there and locate a home.

Half the salary! And we had just bought the new home that Aline loved. Nevertheless, as I talked with Dr. Crose I had an incredible feeling that I would be saying yes. However, I didn't tell him that. I said I'd want to consider the proposition for a few days.

When I weighed the scanty proposal against what Corning had just offered me, it seemed ludicrous.

At that time Corning wanted to send me to Paris for one year. I was to train the Frenchmen at the new Corning plant in all the 126 Corning accounting procedures. They were contained in three thick volumes. I'd be given a sizable salary increase, all my expenses paid for the move and for living in Paris. All our house expenses in the U.S. would be paid too. And I'd have a guarantee that my position and salary would be secured for when I returned.

Besides recently buying my wife's dream home, we had it fixed up with all the extras, the decor, the ambiences, all the little things that made her happy with the home she always wanted. She had arrived. Plus, she led a Bible Study in our home every Monday evening. This exciting group of young married couples, and some singles that age, grew to be over 40 members. She felt responsible for their spiritual growth. How could she leave them? She said it felt like she was being asked to leave her babies. Each one was intimately known and individually dear to her.

Muskogee, Oklahoma was Aline's home from birth. She didn't want to leave her parents, her siblings, her cousins and other relatives as well as the friends she had from years of church and school days. These were her people. She dreaded going to the center of our denominational headquarters where the people were steeped in a different culture and educational climate. Going from life-long friends to complete strangers frightened her. She let me know very firmly that she didn't want to go. But Aline was committed to the Lord long before I was. She knew if we were convinced this was the will of God she would do it regardless of the anxiety and pain. But she resisted with all her might. Perhaps God would not exact it of her.

I wrestled with the decision, considering Aline's personal desires and the timing. As she pointed out, it was winter. Slushy snow with mud was on the ground. It was not the time to sell a house. Besides there were already four houses in our area up for sale with realtor signs on them. They hadn't moved in months.

All these restrictions of Aline's and the "bright yellow carrot" Corning presented us, I thought, was a ploy of the devil to make me break my trusted commitment and keep me from obeying God. Prayerfully and quietly I moved forward. We went to Anderson where we stayed the month with our son who worked there at Anderson University. We located a house, not the one Aline wanted, but one we could afford. We put a down payment on it contingent to our house in Muskogee selling. We went back home and put up a little "For Sale by Owner" sign. Aline and I stood in the yard with our hands on the sign and prayed,

Lord, we're trusting
if it's your will that you will sell this house
so that we can keep the committment
we made to you. Amen

We put a "House for Sale" add in the paper, too. The day the ad came out a young attorney and his family came to see it. They walked through all the rooms, then said, "This is exactly what we have been looking for."

On the spot they bought our house and at our price for cash. There was not one word of negotiation. We called the mover and the day the van left with our belongings, we signed the papers and closed the deal. That night we slept on the floor of the house Aline loved and gave up in obedience to God. Early the next morning we said goodbye to Muskogee and all of our past.

When we got to Anderson, we went to Dr. Sterner's office. There we told him how his sermon caused us to leave our home and come to Anderson to accept the controller's position on the missionary board.

Dr. Sterner threw his hands up into the air. And in excited voice he exclaimed, "Now I know! Now I know! Now I know why God had me preach that sermon. All day I studied on the sermon I was planning to preach. But when I got up to go to the pulpit, God changed my plan. Between my chair and the pulpit I heard God tell me to preach 'God can make you a whole man, physically, mentally and spiritually.'"

With tears running down his face, Dr. Sterner said, "I'm so glad you came to tell me this. I've always wondered why God changed my sermon. I never did that before and I've never done that since."

After that, God further proved to us that we did his will. When I came to the missionary board the indebtedness was deep in the red. In six months we were in the black and throughout the whole eight years I was in the controller's office we remained in the black. At my insistence, all our books were audited by the national Price Waterhouse Auditing Firm, which also audited books for Corning Glass Works. Waterhouse verified that our records were authentic without one negative comment.

Now, after forty-three years, Aline and I are living in a house and neighborhood that is in every way exceedingly beyond our Muskogee home and environment. Here we have a multitude of friends. We've been close enough to our son and his family to watch our grandchildren grow up. Now we have the privilege of snuggling, loving and sharing Jesus with our three oh-so-smart and beautiful great-grandchildren. Aline couldn't be more happy about our move.

God is good—even, when at first, we can't figure it out.

# CHAPTER 16

# Amazing Encounter

## Dr. R. Eugene Sterner

The Communists had just taken over the government in Guyana, South America when I arrived in Georgetown, Guyana. The people were alarmed, resisting the change. Naturally I felt the tension.

It was January of 1971. I was the speaker on our church radio broadcast, The Christian Brotherhood Hour (now View Point). The program was aired by a number of stations in the Caribbean and one in Guyana. I was engaged for a preaching tour among these stations and my last stop was to be in Guyana. The tour went well. The last station was in Georgetown, a strong station with a good listening audience in that English speaking country formerly known as British Guiana.

I applied for entrance. The answer was slow coming. At last I received a very short letter granted me a three-day "work permit." It was made clear that my time was limited.

When I arrived, I saw in the newspaper that one, Forbes Burnham, had seized the bauxite industry. He was the Communist leader. I was concerned about what would be expected of me.

Meetings were to be in the largest church in Georgetown because they were not allowed the use of any public building. When I arrived at the church it was packed full. People were standing all around the outside. It was a huge crowd and we had a good service with a good response. I felt the love of the people. They were all in support of me and what I was there to do.

The next day I was informed I had two appointments. The first was an interview at the radio station. A brash young man, clearly of Communist thought, wondered why I was there. He said we had problems in the United States and pointed out the recent riot in New York City. I said I was there to preach the word of God and to encourage His people. The young man gave me a pretty rough time, but I held my ground. The second appointment was with the former president of Guyana. He was apparently a good man. He kept me for almost an hour, favoring democracy and freedom. He spoke highly of Abraham Lincoln and of our way of life. He told me how he was forced out of office.

My heart ached for him.

The second evening of our meeting there was another huge crowd. A communist official, Minister of Home Affairs, was there. Out of courtesy he was asked to speak. The speech was a tirade against me and what I was doing. He said I was neither needed nor wanted. As he raged on, all I had prepared simply left my mind. I just couldn't remember it. The people started to murmur. The murmuring spread and grew in volume until he was forced to stop.

I was to speak, but I was speechless. By some miracle I remembered a statement made by a French journalist:

> There is neither east nor west,
> Nor border nor breed nor birth
> When two strong men stand face to face
> Though they come from the ends of the earth.

Then I turned to him and said, "I'll meet you on that basis."

Standing at the pulpit I faced the audience—totally without a message. Suddenly, I lost all awareness of where I was and of the people before me.

Some time later, when I came to myself, I was still standing at the pulpit. People were streaming down the aisles to the prayer rooms. I was amazed. I don't know what happened in the between time; but it certainly was none of my doing. It came from a higher power. It had to, to bring that kind of response. It was a powerful act of the Holy Spirit, a victory in the face of Communism. The people marveled at the power of God.

That night I got little sleep. My mind, heart and soul were filled with wonder, love and praise. I couldn't understand it. Obviously, the Spirit of God intervened. I knew that my conscious mind had to have been controlled by the mind of God.

The next and final night the crowd was huge. I was told, on the former night a group of the men escorted the Minister of Home Affairs to his car. I supposed it was for his protection.

Again we had a good service with an encouraging response.

At the close of the final service I was approached by another official of the government. He identified himself as the one in charge of customs. I sensed a different spirit. We talked for a while, then he asked me what time my flight was leaving in the morning.

"I will meet you there at the ticket counter," he said.

Sure enough, he was there.

He ordered my luggage to be checked through. I was relieved and again amazed.

Then, as we stood talking, I felt a deep burden for him. I took him by the arm and led him away from the crowd. There I had the blessed privilege of leading him to the love and grace of God. He was weeping freely.

When my flight was called he walked with me to the gate. His hand caught mine and he squeezed it. I sensed he wanted me to know what he felt in his heart. At the gate we hugged in a warm, brotherly farewell. As I boarded the aircraft I looked back. The last thing I saw of Guyana was this young official, with his hand waving. Again my heart was full of wonder, love and praise.

Although I was filled with awe as I sat in flight, I was also eager to get home to my family. When I did, my wife told me she had asked our three daughters home for a family gathering with me. They came joyously to see their father home safely.

When our daughter Kathy came in, she told me with deep emotion and through tears, "Daddy, I was so burdened for you one night that I had to get out of bed, down on my knees and pray for you till the burden lifted." (She had retired early that evening because she was ill.) I thanked her. And I thanked all of them for their prayers. I thanked God for the love and prayers of my family.

That evening, as I was telling them of my experience in Guyana. Again Kathy spoke up, "Daddy, what time was that?"

We identified the times in the different zones, and as nearly as I could figure, it was the same time I spoke—without knowing what I spoke. Although we were thousands of miles apart, she was led to pray for me at the very time I was under the greatest pressure.

I can't explain it—I don't understand it. One thing I am sure of, it was not of my doing. I can't take the least bit of credit for it. It was God and God alone.

Every person's experience is unique. But I leave you with three words I hope you will never forget: Believe, Obey, and Praise God.

# CHAPTER 17

# A Hand on Mine

## *Jan*

In 1972 my husband, John, was the manager of the First State Bank of Oregon, which is now the Key Bank in down town Milwaukie. This particular morning John woke up with an unbearable headache. He sat on the couch, knowing he couldn't go to work in that condition. I was in the bedroom getting ready to go to a lady's Christmas luncheon when I heard a disturbance in the living room. I rushed out to find John on the floor. He had toppled off the couch and there he lay before me.

In panic, I called our doctor and reached his nurse. Thirty-one years ago there was no 911 emergency call. The nurse said, "I'm sending an ambulance immediately." In five minutes the ambulance was there. John was unconscious. Dwyer Memorial Hospital, now Milwaukie Providence, is only minutes from us. The doctor came as soon as his nurse alerted him. The emergency room was abuzz with activity: getting IV's into John's veins and preparing him for examination.

After the doctor saw John he told me John had had a grand mall seizure. "If I can't bring him out of this coma, you'd better call your family," the doctor warned me. In other words, he was telling me there was little chance of John's survival. I learned later that very few survived a brain hemorrhage such as John had.

I called our family and all our close friends. They came quickly. As soon as I told my very close friend, Evie, she came. Through the December's ice and snow, she came, down on the train from Seattle, Washington. Bless her caring heart, she stayed with me for three days.

John was wheeled into the intensive care unit. Family and friends huddled in a little alcove at the hospital, which was still a small, independently owned facility. There we prayed and lovingly supported each other. When John was settled in intensive care I sat by his bedside and prayed. Our two girls were permitted to come in to see their father whenever they wanted to. For forty eight hours John was in a coma. Then he awakened.

At that time Dwyer Hospital did not have a neurologist on duty nor the equipment for a "cat scan" to examine the brain. For this they took John by ambulance to the Oregon City Hospital, now the Willamette Falls Hospital. At that time, and still today, smaller hospitals cluster together and share their very expensive, specialized equipment. One hospital will invest in one such item while another will invest in a different one. And so they are able to reciprocate.

Only six months earlier, Doctor Stainsby came to Milwaukie from Eugene. How grateful we were to have this fine, highly trained surgeon and caring physician available for John when we so desperately needed him. We felt it was a special blessing from God, for in a short time Dr. Stainsby moved back to Eugene. But, thanks to God, he was here for us.

When people knew John was in need of blood there were volunteers from our church and friends from John's bank.

During John's eight hours of surgery I sat in agonizing fear and deep prayer. While I was holding my Bible and praying, a warm, gentle hand placed itself over mine. The comforting touch lasted only seconds but a peace spread throughout my body. It reached deep inside my mind and heart. I knew God was near. He was with John and he was with me. God's loving, caring Presence was my hope. And thanks to the good Lord and our wonderful Dr. Stainsby, John survived a surgery that few brain-hemorrhage patients ever do.

That night I had an unforgettable dream. John and I were dancing. Yes! we were joyfully dancing. When I awakened I had this firm knowing: my John will make it through this fearful time!

He will make it. I will not lose him. That knowing lodged in my heart and never went away.

Often, while sitting in my chair beside John's bed, I fingered my Bible, letting the pages fall open wherever they would. It was uncanny the way the Bible fell open to the very passage I needed at that moment. Could God or his angels have selected them for me? I felt he did.

For three weeks John was monitored carefully. Infection after surgery could be fatal. Slowly he began to heal.

While John was in the hospital our church, Milwaukie Presbyterian, prayed for him in the services each Sunday. Our friends everywhere were praying continuously. The doctors and nurses all marveled at John's progress. The nurses called him their "Christmas Miracle." They knew how very seldom a patient with such brain hemorrhage survived.

The blow out in John's brain was in the frontal lobe, or the cerebrum, where speech, thought and consciousness reside. Although these were affected, his motor skills were not.

In an aneurysm a blood vessel explodes and destroys that portion of the brain. Whichever abilities are controlled by that area of the brain, those activities of the body are destroyed and by therapy must be rebuilt, if they can be. An aneurysm in the brain is a stroke. In the frontal lobe where John's was it broke down his ability to talk clearly, to read, to do math and other cognizance. After he partially recovered a kindly ex-schoolteacher worked with John and her therapy has allowed him to read, speak clearly, do math and activities of such. However, all his reflexes are much slower than before. Whereas he was a vociferous reader he now reads shorter materials. Long reading causes him brain-fatigue and, with such a piece, at the end he has forgotten the beginning. Short stories and articles he reads and retains very well.

John was only 51 years old when he had the massive stroke. For two years he could not drive a car. Although he was unable to carry on his former responsibilities, Bob and Elsie, these stellar people, then owners of the bank and our good friends, saw John's value as a goodwill-ambassador. They recognized that John's 25 years of caring service had made the bank a multitude of friends. He was given a desk, a secretary when needed, and had the pleasant assignment of serving customers in whatever way he could. When he couldn't help them, he directed them to one who could. Going to work every morning, relating to people all day, having purpose, this was all good therapy for John and speeded his recovery.

Today, thirty one years later, we thank God for the many miracles around John's healing. We celebrate the tremendous gift of still having each other.

And yes, my dream came true. We Are Dancing!

# CHAPTER 18

# Miracles at the Griggs' House

## *David Griggs*

We've had a multitude of faith building miracles at our house. Here are some of them.

### A WHEELCHAIR FOR BABY SCOTT?

We'll start with Scott, our second son. He was born in 1975, on the island of Oahu, Hawaii. He came to us with one foot rotated 90 degrees from normal. The doctors decided to place a cast on the foot, hoping it would correct itself. But once Scott was home from the hospital, I noticed the knee on his other leg seemed different. At first the doctors scoffed at the idea, but later one called and asked to have Scott checked once more. This doctor wasn't sleeping well. Maybe he overlooked something.

Subsequent testing revealed Scott did not have a hip joint on one side. (The other leg had a mis-positioned foot.) The doctors suggested that

Scott would probably never walk. My wife Marcia and I did not have the resources nor the knowledge to question whether there was anything else that could be done.

A close family friend was a Shriner. He thought it wise to see if this fine children's hospital might have a solution. At that time only Shriners could recommend a child for free hospitalization in their organization. Our caring friend gained Scott admission to Shriner's Hospital in Portland, Oregon. Mother Marcia packed up our two kids and headed for Portland.

Shortly after arriving, Marcia attended the Woodstock Church of God in which she'd grown up. A special visiting minister was conducting a healing service. Marcia went forward and asked help for Scott. Prayer was made that Scott's legs would receive divine corrective action or that Marcia would be given grace to live with the situation.

The medical staff at Shriner's were not encouraging. However, they decided to put Scott in a body cast from toes to underarms. This would give the body time to build bones, if that were possible. They were sceptical.

Can you see this baby, prisoner in a cast for a year?

One day the doctors decided to remove the cast and take some X-rays. To their amazement, Scott's skeletal structure was completely normal.

It wasn't long before our little son was walking, running and jumping!

He's a grown man now and has not suffered any affects from his early troubles.

Surely you can imagine how grateful this family is to God and to the Shriner's Hospital staff! We did not have to raise our son with a lifetime confinement to a wheelchair which the first group of doctors predicted and the second group expected.

## NEXT CONSIDER TRAVIS

Travis is our first-born. He came to us in 1972, in Portland, Oregon. It was the middle of the night, and this healthy baby was placed in the infant nursery with dozens of others. Several hours had passed when the best known pediatric doctor in Portland was looking in at his newborns.

He was not responsible for Travis, but happened to glance into Travis' bed. Travis was blue—literally drowning in his mucous. Another minute or two and he'd be gone. The doctor took immediate action. Travis was saved.

Was it mere coincidence that this best known, caring doctor was there at the right time and place—in the middle of the night?

This grateful family doesn't think so.

## HERE'S MARCIA'S STORY

As a young adult, Marcia had her own good fortune.

Her brother's friend built a homemade hydroplane. Several were taking turns driving it around in a lake near Vancouver, Washington. Marcia took her turn, but wasn't ready for that kind of speed or power. She lost control and ran into an off shore island. The boat stopped abruptly. It crashed to pieces and Marcia was launched into the air at high speed. She landed in a huge clump of brush between two large trees.

Protected!

No harm done but—had the trajectory been inches to the left or right the impact on the tree would have broken her neck.

To return to shore, she had to swim through the ice cold lake on a wintry day. Although she was less than 100 feet from shore, she could barely swim. As she struggled through the frigid water, a friend happened on the scene and swam to her. He brought her to safety. She was alive and well!

Praise God!

(We'll say nothing about the hydroplane or it's owner.)

## THEN THERE'S ME, DAVID

I became a Christian in 1980 after years of being completely anti-religious.

One day I was painting the family bathroom with oil based paint.

Although I didn't notice a problem during the effort, that night I became ill. It was just after midnight when I got out of bed for seltzer to calm my stomach. I made it to the living room. There I crumpled on the carpet.

No one knew I was up.

As I lay there, my brain went into high gear assessing my situation. It was clear: I was overcome by breathing the many hours of paint fumes in that small, closed in room. Toxins had poisoned my body—now eating my life away. I lost all sensation. I could think but I couldn't force my eyes to blink. I could not detect any breathing. I tried to hear or feel a heart beat—none. It seemed my body had completely shut down. My brain continued to function. I could reason. I could consider. I was sure I had died.

I began a long dialog with God. My concern was that I had been such a bad example of a functional male. My two sons would not have a chance to develop a healthy image of what a Christian father would be like. I agreed that my whole approach to fatherhood would need to change. A different message should be portrayed. I promised God if he granted me a continuation of life, my family would experience a different person in me.

Suddenly, I heard breath enter my lungs. I noticed a heart beat. Strength began to flow through my veins. Soon I was able to sit up. I felt no sickness. Energy returned and I could lift my body up from the carpet. I went to check the time. It was 6 a m. I had been lying motionless from five to six hours.

New life was mine!

From that moment on I was a different man—far different from what I was before.

Hallelujah, what a savior!

# CHAPTER 19

# God's Reconstruction Job

## *A. H.*

It was in Tacoma, Washington, back in the late forties, that I was given the greatest miracle of my life. I didn't know I needed it, but God began a serious work on me.

Although I was only twenty-six years old, my problems seemed insurmountable. I was frustrated and depressed to the extent that I didn't want to live. I thought of walking a narrow highway close to our house where huge commercial trucks came swooshing by. If one hit me just right, that would be a legitimate way to end my misery.

I called on God and begged him to solve my problems. He didn't. He just let me become sicker than I was, physically and emotionally: so sick, I had to go to bed and stay there for more days than I can remember. How could I care for my two small children? None of my family was near to help. I felt my husband wasn't doing a thorough job of it.

Doctor after doctor did not diagnose my case. All they told me was that I had a cold. One time when a doctor told me that, I was tempted to ask for my $5.00 back, since I knew that diagnosis before I made the appointment.

There on my bed I lay. No, I couldn't lie down. I choked when I did. I was propped up in bed with pillows. The pain in my abdomen doubled me up. Bronchial infection caused severe and continual day and night coughing. Flu like symptoms made my body weak and aching all over. Medical prescriptions were useless.

In a very respectable, orthodox manner I prayed and asked God to heal me. When that failed, I began to demand it, using the terms, "In Jesus name!" "As the Word says," "God, you promised," "By your stripes I am healed." These were biblical sayings I had heard for years.

With that level of prayer exhausted (my patience as well), I told God just how I felt. If he were the loving heavenly Father we were taught he was, wouldn't he be more compassionate? Wouldn't he heal his child? If my child were suffering as I was, I would do all I could to remove the pain and heal him. Could I be more caring than he, God was? Does he even know me, individually?

If God is everywhere, I reasoned, then he was standing at my bedroom door seeing me suffer. Obviously, he didn't care enough to do anything for me.

I was a pastor's wife and a Sunday school teacher. I taught my class that God was an all loving, caring God, always with us, as in Matthew 28:20b. "...and, lo, I am with you always, even to the end of the world." Maybe that meant to the ends of the earth if I were a missionary carrying the gospel. Maybe that didn't mean in my bedroom with me when I was sick.

The Lord's Prayer taught us to say, "Our Father, which art in heaven." I said it over and over, more times than I could count. But now I wondered if he really was the kind of God I believed in and taught. Maybe he is that harsh judging one I always hoped he wasn't. Maybe he wants me to suffer for all the sins I have committed. They weren't big carnal sins because I tried from my youth up to obey his Word. But I was resentful, impatient, often angry and just then, disrespectful and indignant.

After exhausting myself with pleading and begging and demanding prayers, I began to envision a faraway God, a generally uncaring, non-compassionate power, unconcerned with his creation's sufferings. I myself was more compassionate toward those I loved.

More and more, I became angry at God. He wasn't doing a thing for me. Hadn't I tried to serve him faithfully all my twenty-some years? My anger and self-pity mounted.

When I became aware of how impatient, irritated, angry and irreverent I was toward God, I was shocked awake. Why, if I talked that way to my mother, her backhand would have known no mercy. And here I was, talking that way to God!

Seeing my impudence, I repented in utter humility.

"Oh, God, forgive me. I don't blame you for not healing me. I don't deserve it. I deserve to suffer even worse. I'm a selfish, bratty kid: belligerent, smart-mouthed, disrespectful, impatient, irritable. Cleanse me, Lord. And please, dear Jesus, teach me to pray."

At that moment I realized I knew how to say words at God but I knew little about effective prayer.

I had my husband, Sam, get me several books on the subject of prayer. O. Holsby's book entitled *Prayer* was very helpful. But the greatest help came from E. Stanley Jones' little volume, *Abundant Living*. The prayer section begins on page 224. That page is sacred in my memory.

E. Stanley Jones told me to listen to God. To put God at the center of my attention. He said God wanted the best for us. We might think what we want is good. But God wants better. Our good could block God's better.

Dr. Jones challenged me to try to think of God for five minutes without referring to myself. I couldn't. That, he said, proved how self-centered I was.

Listen, learn, obey, Jones said, was the formula for abundant living. Abundant living was what I wanted. I dedicated myself to the disciplines that would lead me there: listening to God and striving to bring my emotions under his control.

Dr. Jones told me I couldn't live spiritually without eating any more than I could live physically without eating. So the Bible became my daily bread. Jones talked about taking daily nourishment by having a "Quiet Time," as he called daily devotions. I liked the term and adopted it. From then on it was my name for the tryst I held with God.

As I became more and more aware of the goodness of God I grew less and less concerned with my health. I was willing to learn patience and endurance.

"Endure hardship as a good soldier," I read in my Bible (2nd Tim. 2:3), which I started to read hungrily.

With my attention focused on spiritual health, I hardly realized I was gaining physical strength day by day. Soon I was able to be up short periods of time. Then longer and longer. After some weeks I could stand up straight without abdominal pain. Coughing had subsided. My head cleared, I was on my way to wellness! More importantly, I was gaining spiritual health.

Now I wanted to die to my selfish ways and my self-centered living. I wanted to grow strong in spirit and learn to "walk with God." Each morning I rose a half hour before the family to have my designated "Quiet Time." Soon this stretched into an hour. Before long I quit counting minutes and gave my attention to communicating with my new found love, the Lord Jesus Christ.

Thus began my spiritual adventure. Many excursions we took together, God and I. There were still some rugged mountains to climb. But the journey became lighter and the relationship with Jesus has now become my life's greatest joy. Because of this mental, emotional and spiritual healing, I have had a wonderful, adventurous life with a multitude of exciting and memorable experiences.

Here is a poem I wrote recently.

COMPANIONS

I talk with God
In the stillness of my heart.
I walk with God
In the pathways of my mind.
He talks to me of his gifts
of love and life.
He walks with me
And guides my feet aright.

Ever present
He sustains me
In the sunshine of my days
And the shadows of my night.

What greater healing could I ask for?

# CHAPTER 20

# Attitude Adjustment

## *A. H.*

Can such a little, insignificant thing as an attitude adjustment be a miracle? I don't know. You judge. Although it's a small incident, it changed my life in a big way.

In E. Stanley Jones' book *Abundant Living* he gave me so many jewels. One of them was "Listen, Learn, Obey." For years that has served me bountifully. I have trained myself to listen for God's voice within. Many spiritual writers speak of "that still, small voice that whispers to the soul." You'll miss it if you're too consumed with the clamor of outward happenings.

There's another gem I received from my wise mentor. It is this insightful statement: "What gets your attention gets you."

Oh, how many years I've practiced that one! I've taken inventory of my interests, faced up to the truth of what I let my mind dwell on, sifted out that which I knew was not pleasing to the one I profess to serve, love, obey and have guiding my life—Jesus.

Well, a significant/insignificant thing happened recently.

I was sitting at my computer working on this manuscript. I looked out the window and saw Sam drive away in his cherished, old 1997 Chev Lumina van (8 years old at this time). I just knew he was going to Taco Bell to get us each two or three tacos. The more I thought on it the more my hunger kicked in and the more my tasters adjusted to a spicy bit of hamburger in a crisp, corn shell with lettuce, tomato and mild taco sauce poured over. No doubt Sam would bring cold Pepsi, too.

I stayed at my computer, working diligently. But for a half hour my mind flashed to a spicy taco. I knew I'd have a good meal when Sam came back. I had time to work up an appetite while imagining the aroma of Tacos. Mexican is my favorite food next to home-fried-chicken with mashed potatoes and gravy.

When Sam got back I listened and grinned to myself. I'm in for a treat.

Soon I heard his voice, "Honey, would you like something to eat?"

"I'll be right there," I said.

But my mind said, "Would I?! I want those tacos you brought.

I hurried from my computer room which is in "the back forties" of our house. I rushed out, through my bedroom, the utility room, the kitchen and into the dinning area to stand at the side of the table, expecting—you know what!

There on a pretty plate on a colorful place mat, across the table from Sam, lay a—slice of watermelon.

Watermelon! I thought. I don't want watermelon! I want tacos!

I felt like following the example of our little twenty-month-old great granddaughter when she doesn't get what she wants. I could see myself, an eighty-four-year-old, kinda fat woman lying on the floor crying, kicking, screaming, "I want tacos!"

I'm not even going to imagine what Sam would do with that. I put fretfulness out my mind—quickly and replace it with another attitude. (What gets your attention gets you—remember?.)

I could have grunted and said, "Shucks, Honey, I thought you were bringing tacos."

But after practicing the "attitude game" for many years, I knew the choice was mine. Would I be positive or negative? Would I be grateful or unappreciative? Would I act pleasingly or begrudgingly?

Consciously I chose and did a quick turn over.

I looked at my husband, so delighted with himself for getting me that beautiful, delicious, marvelous, piece of nature's late-summer bounty. This loving man of mine went to the store and brought us a watermelon.

I used the attitude adjustment skills I learned throughout the years by practicing Dr. Jones' mentoring. I would be appreciative and make peace and joy reign in our house.

Thanks to God's and Dr. E. Stanley Jones' ever-living-truths, I swallowed my wants and turned my attention to the beautiful, rich, red, white and green piece of fruit which, by the many miracles of mother nature and human ingenuity, sat before me and to this good man who lovingly cares for me. I ate watermelon and enjoyed the company of my healthy, loving, living, eighty-six-year-old husband.

By the way, he always eats his melon from the heart out. I start from the sides and work in. That makes the heart an extra treat for me. Now, I must confess, that's a pretty accurate picture of Sam and me. In most everything, we come from opposite ends. Now you know, that could make for serious difficulties. And it would, but for this tiny miracle of attitude change that makes a big difference in how we choose to live our every day lives.

# CHAPTER 21

# Angel in Uniform

## *Kim Raichl*

It was in June, during the Rose Festival in Portland, Oregon. There was a big amusement park situated near the Willamette River. My six-year-old son, Nathan, and his buddy Oaks, were determined to go to the park and have fun on all those rides. They talked about it for days. I was working down town so Oaks' father said he'd take the boys to the park. We agreed that I'd meet them there after I got off work at five o'clock.

The only place I found to park was on the other side of a six lane, busy highway. To get to the river side I had to go through a long, dark tunnel that went under the road near the Broadway bridge. I stood near the mouth of the tunnel and shivered. In the gloom I could see some scruffy looking guys hanging out in the tunnel. I badly needed to go on to meet my son and his buddies. But I was dreadfully afraid to step into that tunnel. I stood half frozen for several minutes and then made myself take a step into the darkness.

With that first step I heard a footstep beside me. Then another and another. I glanced out of the side of my eye and saw—there walked a tall, slender, very handsome policeman in full uniform. I was so stunned I couldn't even look around let alone utter a sound. He didn't say a word either. Side by side we cruised right past the "sure enough, four-very-hard-looking guys." At the end of the tunnel when I stepped into the daylight, I turned my head to look at my partner. I thought he might even want my telephone number. I was single and available. He was so very handsome and well poised.

But he wasn't there. I searched the area immediately around me and then out in a wider area. No one! Not another person was near. My handsome policeman evaporated into thin air. Was he my guardian angel materialized? Or was he a special miracle of God sent to protect me? I wish I knew. And I wish I could have given him my telephone number.

# CHAPTER 22

# Give Thanks, in a Robbery?

## *A. H.*

Nick, our grandson, hugged Sam and me as he greeted us at the airport on our return to Portland from a five-day visit to Joplin, Missouri. As we rolled down the highway toward home he said, "Well, I'm going to get right to serious business with you. You've been robbed. Both of our houses were broken into and your cars are gone. Your garage and carport are empty."

What a shock!

When we walked into the house, my anxiety mounted. The floors were strewn with clothes and papers. Empty drawers indicated a search for money. The scene in the bedroom was most frightening. Just three feet from Sam's side of the bed, outside the jimmied glass door lay an ax, a hammer, a crow bar, and a carpenter's claw. If that didn't scare us nothing would! What if we'd been home?

How could God let this happen to us? Where were our guardian angels? I wondered.

Sam's study was torn up, too. His file marked "Automobile" which held the titles and service records to the two cars was gone. So they had the titles to both cars and the key rings. These had our house keys on them. They had keys to all our locks! That was an alarming thought.

I ran into the living room to see if the robbers had damaged my prized, antique, French, China cabinet with its delicate curved glass doors, intricate inlaid wood, and exquisite French finish.

"Thank you, God!" I exclaimed when I saw it intact, with its contents of cut glass and valuable figurines. I added our four antique clocks to my investigation. I was relieved to see that the great grandmother clock, standing eight feet tall, which our children brought us from Berlin, Germany, was untouched. A scurry into other rooms assured me the burglars didn't take our VCR and two TVs. That was strange but good. My biggest sigh of relief came when I found they didn't touch my study with it's computer, printer, fax machine and loaded files. Devastation to my writing projects would have cut me down to bitter sobbing.

"Thank you, God! Oh, thank you, God!" I cried with elation. "And I even feel some gratitude toward the wretched robbers!" I said.

The police asked me to make a list of the missing items: a gold and diamond pendant on a heavy gold chain, a gift from my sister; an emerald ring which Sam gave me for my seventy-fifth birthday; a '91 Cadillac, which Sam's blind sister gave to Sam, after her husband died; an '89 Mercedes that Jeni, my daughter-in-law, gave me when she received a new BMW as a Christmas gift from Randy, our son. These were only a few of the items.

My former eagerness to be home and in my own bed waned when I realized the burglars had our house keys. The police relieved my mind some by telling us, "We've never known of robbers coming right back. They know the occupants would probably be waiting for them with a gun."

When I considered it rationally I thought, Sure, why should they come back? They got everything they wanted the first time?

So, I crawled into bed next to Sam, my great protector, and slept peacefully.

The next day, greatly relieved that my study was intact, I said to Sam, (in light hearted jest, of course) "I think I'll write a thank you note to the robbers and put it in the Oregonian (newspaper) telling them how grateful I am for (1) They didn't trash out our house. Messed it up, yes, but trashed, no. (2) They came when we were away, saving us the trauma of being caught in a scene with burglars. (3) They took things with sentimental value, yes—but things, the loss of which didn't give us trauma or great emotional pain. (4) Although we loved our cars, they were older, 1989 and '9—in 2001. Maybe it was time we upgraded."

Of course I was kidding. But after the insurance was collected for the cars, jewelry and other items, we had money enough to buy two newer cars, a tiny miracle in itself. So we did have quite a bit to give thanks for, even in a robbery.

# CHAPTER 23

# Sufficient Grace

## *A. H.*

It was hard for me to see my very good friend, Aline Fair, suffer so. After seven years of post herpetic neuralgia (nerve damage from shingles), it still felt like an animal clawing at her upper chest and back. She told me the nearly unbearable pain never lets up. Of all the different pain killers the doctors prescribed, none brought relief. Added to this trauma, Aline had severe arthritis in her knees. Her left knee was replaced. Her right knee, with bone grinding on bone, also needed replacement. She can't bring herself to accept more suffering.

Then several near tragic things happened to her. The most life threatening was a burst diverticula which sent poison throughout Aline's body with peritonitis beginning to set in. Writhing in pain, she was rushed to the hospital for immediate surgery. Had she waited 24 hours she would have died, the doctor said. Her incision was from the pelvis to the navel plus an opening for a colostomy. Ten inches were removed from her colon. An abscess developed where the colon was stapled together. Again infection brought her close to death.

After thirty days in the hospital, arthritis besieged her hips.

Some time later, Sam and I, Grant and Pam, our son and daughter-in-law, visited her and her husband Denton. Wherever we went, uncomplaining, Aline walked along in her hobbling way. I was amazed at her patience, acceptance, and endurance.

For fifty-five years Aline and I had been closest friends. Our friendship was forged out of steel: our own mettle of stubborn characters and God's anvil and hammer of discipline. We were in our search for life in Christ together and it welded us as one. The blows of criticism and the rotten eggs of disdain were not able to drive us apart. We knew what God had already done for us and we wanted to be obedient to all he asked of us. God's discipline was exacting. We knew his purpose was to bring us to life and life abundant. The great joy of release and rejuvenation were too precious to jeopardize.

Although, at this time, we lived two thousand miles apart we were still one in spirit. She tells her friends, "Adele's my spiritual mother." I reply, "And she's my beautiful spiritual child." The truth is we both suffered labor pains and persecution to gain our "life in Christ." We committed ourselves to be bondservants of our Lord Jesus. And we understood much of what that phrase meant.

Now, here we were, Sam and I, guests at the Fair's house. It was early morning. Lying in bed, I was contemplating the pain and suffering of this one who was so dear to my heart. We were spiritual sisters, perhaps twins. I hurt as though her wounds were mine. In agony of spirit I called on God, "Why, oh why, do you let this faithful and loving child of yours suffer so?"

Further contemplating her heroic endurance and patient suffering, my pain turned to grief. I wept with heart-tearing pain.

Then I heard God speak to my mind, "Do not grieve so. She is showing forth my grace in suffering."

I was stunned!

Letting my mind go into God's presence, I heard him again, "Look at her as she walks among my people."

In vision I could see Aline walking among people: at church, to special events, to weddings, anniversary celebrations, to birthday parties.

"Look at you," they'd say, astonished at her presence there. "You're so pretty. You're beautiful!"

I could hear God say, "This is the beauty of the Christ Spirit as it radiates from her. People who know her, know her pain and they see her bearing it lovingly and with grace. She is a witness to my grace in suffering."

When our husbands were gone to a meeting and Aline and I were alone, visiting, I said, "Aline, God talked to me this morning."

"What did He say to you, Adele?" Aline asked.

I proceeded to tell her how, in the very early morning, I was praying and suffering grief for her in her terrible pain.

"And Aline, God said, 'Do not grieve. She is bearing my wounds in her flesh and thereby showing forth my grace in suffering. Those who have eyes to see, will see and know—my grace is sufficient.'

"Aline, I hesitate to tell you this but I felt God said you are his willing servant and he has called you to serve in this way."

"Adele," Aline replied, "I believe that. If I didn't believe that, I couldn't bear this pain. I'd give up and not try to keep going. You know I can hardly walk. For years I prayed those words of the Apostle Paul, 'That I might know him, and the power of his resurrection, and the fellowship of his suffering, being made conformable unto his death.' Now if God is fulfilling that prayer in my life, who am I to complain? When I'm alone I sing this song,

Lord I fellowship thy passion.
Gladly suffer pain and loss.
In thy blessed pain is pleasure.
I will glory in the cross.
It is that, that keeps me going."

I bowed my head in humility and tearfully prayed,

Lord, help me remember this moment.
And the next time I pray and pray for healing
with no results, remind me
that you may well be using my suffering
for redemptive purpose.
May I too surrender to your will—
without complaining.

# CHAPTER 24

# God Gave Us Our Mama Back

## *A. H.*

It was during our family's early years in Medicine Hat, Canada, that Mama became sick nigh unto death with edema. She was hospitalized until the doctor told Papa to come get her. He said, "We've done all we can for your wife. And you can't afford for us to keep her. She might as well die at home."

The pastor's wife, Sister Arbeiter, as she was called, told Papa, "Bring Lydia here. You have all those children to care for, I'll take care of Lydia."

In an upstairs room of the pastor's home, Mama lay waiting to die. Brother Arbeiter visited Mama daily and had prayer with her. He gave her Bible Scriptures to read and told her if she had faith, God would heal her.

It was hard for Mama to believe she could be healed. But with constant encouragement and the prayers of the small congregation that met in the pastor's home, finally Mama gained courage. Brother Arbeiter told Mama, "You pray and talk to God about it and when you're ready let me know and we'll anoint you (with oil, according to the Scripture) and pray for you."

One Saturday night Mama told her pastor she was ready for that anointing and prayer. He said, "All right, tomorrow after service we'll pray for you." Which they did.

The men carried Mama on a cot down into the meeting room. The congregants gathered around her. Pastor Arbeiter anointed Mama's forehead with blessed oil and laid his hand on her head. All the people reached out to touch Mama. Then the pastor prayed a simple prayer asking God to touch this, His child, and heal her.

Mama said a shock as of lightning shot through her body, from the top of her head to the toes of her feet. She jumped up and shouted, "I'm healed, I'm healed."

A friend of Mama's lived across the street from the pastor's house. She too was sick. Excited Mama, in her gown and robe, ran across the street to the woman's house and said, "I'm healed! I'm healed! And God can heal you, too."

The woman responded sarcastically, "Lydia, you're crazy. Go back to bed or you're going to drop dead in your tracks." This, of course, all went on in German. I may not be an accurate translator but the message is accurate.

From then on, Mama was rid of that disease. She came back home and took care of her family, working like a horse, as she always did.

# CHAPTER 25

# Divine Anesthetist

## *A. H.*

One of the most memorable happenings of my childhood was when Papa fell off the house roof. We moved to the country because he had a weak heart. From the way he worked you'd never have known it. But when he fell off the roof and broke his leg the doctors feared to set it because they said his heart wouldn't stand the shock.

The thigh bone splintered and the impact of the fall drove the lower part of the splintered bone up into the muscle two inches. To set the leg they would have to pull the two pieces of bone apart to bring the ends together. (Maybe even cut the splinters off.) Doctors would put a pin through the leg to hold the bone pieces in place and raise the leg with a weight at the end of a pulley until the leg began to heal.

Daddy's doctor called in other doctors for consultation. Then they told Mama, "We have a dilemma. Your husband's heart is so weak that we can't give him anesthesia. It will kill him. If we operate without anesthesia, the pain will be too much for his heart. If we don't set the leg gangrene will set in and we'll have to amputate. That would put us in the same dilemma we are in now. We just don't know what to do. Every way we turn we see losing him."

Mama said, "Let me tell my husband."

She told Daddy and Daddy said, "Mama, let's pray."

They prayed and Daddy said, "Tell the doctors to operate."

Mama told them, "My husband said for you to operate. We have faith that God will see him through."

Mama stood by Daddy's head and prayed. Daddy waited for the doctors to begin. A nurse came to cover Daddy's eyes but he brushed the cloth away. He waited. And he waited more. Finally he was impatient and said, "Mama, tell the doctor to go ahead, I'm ready."

They waited longer. Again Daddy said, "Mama, tell the doctor I'm ready."

When Mama relayed the message, the doctor said, "We're through."

They made the complicated operation; pulled the splintered bones apart and lined them up, inserted the steel pin the size of one's index finger, wheeled him into his room, hitched him up to the contraption that hoists the leg into the air, put the weight at the foot-end to give tension, and Papa never felt one pang of pain.

Again our family had a miracle—a big one. Daddy's surgery without anesthesia was as great as Mama's healing of edema.

How can any of us Gwinner kids be doubters? How can we not believe in a God who can be called and called until he gives his good blessing?

We, as a family, sure did hassle God a lot.

Along with Mama's and Daddy's problems, like most families we had many severe ailments. Emily, as a child, had scarlet fever which left her nearly deaf. Anita had scarlet fever, too. The doctors said she'd always have a weak heart. Lydia almost chopped her big toe off. Al nearly died of double pneumonia. Herb nearly chopped his thumb off. Ollie was always sickly. It's a wonder she grew up. In Lydia's adult years she had seven major operations. Several years ago I had arthritis so badly I could hardly walk two blocks. I was bound for hip replacement or a wheelchair.

In fact, I went to Disneyland with our daughter Marydith and grandson, Joshua. Marydith got a wheelchair for me and pushed me around in it. Now, thanks to God and the wonderful nutritional supplements I take called "Reliv," I'm without pain for the first time in over thirty years. I've not had hip surgery and most every morning Sam and I walk at the Clackamas Town Center Mall.

Lydia, in her retirement, played nine holes of golf every morning. If Anita had a weak heart from her bout with scarlet fever, God healed her because she works like a horse and hasn't had any sign of after effects. Al grew up healthy and strong as an ox.

Too, when Al was real little he got himself locked in the horse barn and he declares an angel opened the door for him. Our family has had so many miracles we couldn't count them all. I think Mama's prayers saved us all from devastating affects.

To me the biggest miracle is that eight of us kids grew up to be fine Christian adults. We joke about one of Mama's sayings, "I have all good children. None of them have ever been in jail." And that's a miracle in itself. We were all mischievous, maybe even ornery, sometimes lacking strict morals. But by the grace of God we made it! And I'm sure we'll all meet Mama and Daddy in heaven.

Hurrah for you, God!

And hurrah for you, Mama. Thanks for your prayers and for the way you worked and suffered for us. Daddy, thanks for your faithfulness to our big family and for your hard work.

# CHAPTER 26

# A Flying Car?

## *Anita Merrill*

I was driving home on 185th street in Beaverton, Oregon. My daughter, Kim, was in the seat beside me and her baby, Nathan, was in his car seat behind us.

185th street crosses a railroad track. At this time there was a big bump in the road there. It was hazardous. Usually cars drove slowly and carefully because there was a stop sign immediately at the bottom of the hill. There I was stopped behind two cars.

A car must have been coming over the tracks at breakneck speed for I heard a loud crashing sound. I looked around. Out the rear window I saw a big, old-model car come sailing, air borne, right toward the rear of our car. I knew it could do nothing but hit us.

He'll smash our baby and kill us, too, my mind flashed. There's no place I can rush to, to get out of his way, I'm behind two more cars. We're doomed!

Something in me shouted, "God save us!"

Later, I distinctly remembered thinking, Where did that come from? I didn't think it up.

Now I realize it must have been the Holy Spirit in me who prayed that instant prayer.

The car, sailing through the air, crash-landed on it's wheels no more than eight inches from our rear bumper. Then it bounced straight up again. Air borne, it turned over onto it's top. Still upside-down, it flew across the road and landed in a ditch. The driver walked away, dazed but unharmed.

For that car, air borne, to land within eight inches of our car and not crash into us was a miracle. For that car to lift straight up into the air again, without touching our car, was a miracle. For our little one to have been that close to being killed and yet not scratched, was a miracle. For Kim and me to escape the injury of our car slamming into the car in front of us, that was a miracle. In fact, that a prayer came out of my mouth that I didn't even have time or thought to pray, was a miracle.

We three, Nathan, Kim and I, are here today by the many-miracled graces of God.

# CHAPTER 27

# Rescue from Parsimony

*A. H.*

I grew up in the deep depression. Many people went hungry. Fathers were out of work or on WPA, which was Roosevelt's "Government Work Project Association." We had a farm and grew our food so we ate well. But Mama and Daddy were deep in debt. The worry in our household was as thick and heavy as Oregon's deepest fog. It affected my thinking: conscious and subconscious. I became very saving.

I saved everything: strings, pins, bobby pins with both protective ends off. They were sharp, scratched my head, stuck my scalp, and broke my hair. But I endured it all and much, much more for thrift's sake.

I became very adept with a rubber spatula, scraping every inch of a mixing bowl or pan. I threw little away, never sent old clothes to Good Will or Salvation Army, shopped there instead. It was not easy for me to spend or to give. I paid my 10% tithe to the church. That, I felt, was my religious duty. But, of course, I expected God to give it back and just maybe with interest.

Then one day I read an essay by Thomas Jefferson in which he spoke of parsimony as one of the seven deadly sins. Parsimony—greed, stinginess! Could I be stingy? I thought thrift was a virtue!

I must have begun discussing this with God. Because I became acutely aware of my discomfort in giving when opportunities came to me. I began considering the act of giving. I decided to adventure a little ways down this road. I did, haltingly. When I gave it was with calculated precision—not too much but not too little to be called stingy. I struggled with how much was precisely right.

Then one day God talked to me about another subject—the beauty of generosity. He made generosity look like a rare and precious flower growing in the garden of my soul. He showed me, in my mind's eye, how beautiful my garden would be if I planted a whole separate and special garden of roses. It started me desiring the beauty of generosity even while I laughed at the thought. It was so foreign to my growing-up. It made me feel a bit naked. But it seemed quite intriguing.

I started out slow, finding good buys and making them gifts. Oh, I never paid full price for anything. If I wanted a particular something I'd wait for it to be on sale. I still do. But then Jesus showed me a place I could exercise my new virtue and feel good about it—"Missions!"

Here I could give small offerings to missionaries through my church.

Then I took a big step. I gave $15.00 to buy a goat for the poor people in Peru. I felt I'd made it! It didn't even hurt.

In fact, it was fun! I could see the little goat prancing around, playing with the children. It might even have a love affair with another goat and start a family of baby goats. In time, many families in Peru might have goat milk for their children. What a rewarding thought!

The more I contemplated it, the greater the joy of giving grew for me. Now, after many years of this exercise of the soul-muscle, it's some of the most fun I have.

Can giving become addictive?

# CHAPTER 28

# In Total Fright

*name withheld*

At thirty-two years of age I was drafted into the U.S. Army's Second World War. For training I was sent from Portland, Oregon to the deep South—Louisiana. For me, the differences made quite a cultural shock. But when I decided to attend a certain church, I got the shock of a lifetime.

I often heard about a church where the people were called "snake handlers." I was told they took the last part of the gospel of Mark in a literal way—and to an astounding degree. From this Scripture they quoted Jesus saying, "They shall take up snakes."

"They will be able to handle snakes with safety," another translation says. These people, I was told, were actually handling snakes in their worship services.

I could hardly believe it, but I was curious. I'll go see for myself what it's all about, I thought. So I did.

The little ramshackle building seemed more like a shack than a church.

When I entered, the minister was preaching. The minister then led the people in prayer. Many of them started praying out loud, all at the same time. Being brought up a quiet Quaker, I was stunned. This, in itself, was foreign to me and the music was loud and jivey. The piano banged away with plenty of rhythm. The people started dancing while they shouted their prayers. To me it was bedlam. Some, like me, were silent. This is as foreign to worship as it can get, I thought.

Soon two ministers went out and came back with gunny sacks over their shoulders. These they dropped to the floor and shook. Snakes of all kinds slithered away. I quaked! But not in holy awe! I quaked in ungodly fright. I would have lunged for the back door but there was a man covering it. Each door had a guard.

We were told that we could not leave until we entered into the act of faith by picking up a snake.

For several minutes I watched the two ministers as they handled snakes, one in each hand. The snakes crawl over them, around their necks, down their arms, even across their faces. I saw the ministers kiss the snakes' mouths. Ugh!

What kind of snakes were these? Little green garter snakes? Oh no! These were wild snakes caught right there out of the southern hills where they have deadly copperheads, cotton mouths, water moccasins and rattlesnakes. I knew rattlers were among them and I was determined to get out of that shocking, ghastly, macabre place.

I saw a big rattlesnake slithering past me. Quickly I grabbed it by the tail, just in front of the rattlers. For a split second I held it out at arm's length and flung it down. In dire fright, I jumped over the snakes around me and bolted out the door. With great relief, back in my sane, safe world, I breathed God's free air.

I've never forgotten this shivering experience of sixty years ago. I still don't understand the power these people had over the snakes. I know they felt it was their faith in this Scripture, Mark 16:18,* that God will protect them from harm even if they pick up snakes. But personally, I have no sympathy with a people showing their faith in God in such an outlandish and bizaare way. Of course, I'm not God, so I'll let God judge them and withhold mine.

You may ask, "Where's the miracle in all of this?" To me, the miracle is that I got out of there alive!

*Translations differ with Mark 16. Some give a short version, ending with the 8th verse. Others have the long ending through verse 20.

# CHAPTER 29

# Angels Came

*Ron Palmer*

Springtime in Palouse Country of Eastern Washington is breathtakingly beautiful with its many-shaded fields of new grain.

But our thoughts were far from Mother Nature's beauty. Just the opposite. Our minds were filled with grief and near tragedy. We were on our way from Moscow, Idaho to Portland, Oregon. There my wife, Ruth, would take a flight to Minneapolis to attend her 15-month-old nephew's funeral.

I was driving the car when suddenly I doubled up with excruciating pain.

A farmhouse stood in the middle of a grain field. Ruth drove me there and the kind people let us call an ambulance.

I was rushed to My Lady Of Lourdes Hospital in Pasco, Washington. Here I underwent more tests and procedures than I can remember. The morphine that should have controlled the pain had little or no effect. My skin and eyes were yellow. The doctor foresaw that testing would take several days. (My hospital stay stretched out to twenty-eight days.)

Ruth, torn between not wanting to leave me so ill and the desire to be with her grieving family, reluctantly took the doctor's advice and left to join her family.

In spite of the many times before that I'd been rushed to the doctor or the hospital's emergency room, my old ailment had never been diagnosed. Test after test, treatment after treatment and medication after medication all failed.

Now, after two days of tests, pictures, poking and prodding, it was determined my gallbladder had petrified and was filled with hundreds of small, crystallized stones. This gravel was too small to be detected readily on a screen. Surgery was mandatory.

The days ahead were a blur of excruciating pain, fever, tubes and hallucinations. Even after the surgery, my condition grew increasingly worse. I became critical. Specialists were called in to help save me. It was finally determined that pancreatitis had developed.

The pancreas is a pinkish-yellow organ about six to eight inches long, an-inch-and-a-half wide and a half-inch thick. It lies crosswise behind the stomach and is looped by the duodenum, the first part of the small intestine. This gland releases digestive juices and insulin into the intestines. My pancreas was infected, inflamed, and sending poison throughout my body.

During this time, although I was in too much pain to think, there was a constant inner sense that God loved me, my family loved me and my church was praying for me.

One Tuesday when I was so desperately ill, a dear, older man of God, Lloyd Skramstad, felt led to come visit me. Earlier, he was in our congregation in Moscow and now lived in Walla Walla, Washington. Because he and his wife had had an adult foster care, he was experienced with the sick and dying. From all my symptoms, Lloyd believed I was dying.

He stayed with me all day and evening until the nurse said visiting hours were over. She came to my room and told Lloyd, "Unless you're family, you have to leave."

"I'm family," Lloyd said.

He stayed.

Lloyd sat by my bedside all night. Here he watched over me and prayed continuously that God would save me. Several times Lloyd saw I was in severe trouble and quickly alerted the nurse. Had he not been there, no doubt I would have died. The next day when Ruth came into my room, there sat Lloyd. Like an angel he never left my side. He stayed on watch throughout the night until another angel came to watch and pray.

The pancreas produced so much infection it was attacking other organs. Another surgery was performed, this time to treat the pancreas and the infected area around it. The infection had also spread to the liver and spotted it. Part of the liver was removed. The doctor told Ruth that twice I was near death. Now, with IV's and six to seven bags of medications going into veins through both arms, I began to make slow, painful progress. The incision was left open to heal from the inside outward. This meant the wound had to be cleansed and dressed regularly. After 28 days I was released. My poor wife took on the unpleasant jobs.

Too weak, in the hospital, to help myself and often overcome with depression, God sent angels to watch over me in my darkest hours. I must remember to request of God a halo for my gracious, caring friend, Lloyd Skramstad and wings for my patient, loving, enduring, comforting wife, Ruth. It's due to them, with the help of earnest and sincere doctors, the goodness of God and the prayers of many dear people of God that I am alive today. All working together afforded me a lifesaving miracle.

# CHAPTER 30

# A Month of Wondrous Grace

## *A. H.*

In January, 2001, my husband Sam and I had happenings piled on top of happenings, all packed into thirty days. It was an endurance contest that started with an alert from Sam's nephew Bob Loudermilk, in Joplin, Missouri. Bob's mother and Sam's sister, had yet another stroke. She was not able to swallow food or water and didn't recognize family or friends. She had long been ailing and eager to "go home." The children wisely elected not to hook her up to life support at ninety-one years of age. Sam and I readied ourselves for a flight at a moment's notice. That notice soon came and we flew from Portland, Oregon to Joplin, Missouri, where Sam officiated his sister's funeral.

When we returned, as you read in Chapter 22, "GIVE THANKS" IN A ROBBERY? we learned our house was robbed and both cars stollen. My first reminder of God's grace was that we weren't home at the time of the robbery. The second came when I realized I could say a prayer, snuggle up to Sam and go peacefully to sleep with a messed up house, a broken sliding-glass door into our bedroom and robbers having our house keys. That was a "Praise God." Of course, the police told us robbers rarely come right back, knowing the owners would be alert and waiting with a gun.

But that all this could happen without throwing us into an emotional frenzy was only by our faith and the grace of God.

We had the work of cleaning up after the robbers, fixing the broken sliding-glass door, changing all the locks on the house, making a list of missing things and filing the police report.

We had interviews with the insurance people, forms to fill out, a car to rent and two cars to shop for. This all took time.

"Thank you God, for adequate insurance!" Another grace.

Our second day home, we got a call from my niece, Darlene Goin. The conversation went like this.

Darlene: "Ardy, (her husband) is in the hospital again. I thought you'd want to know."

Me: "Of course. We want to come! But we have two appointments. We could come to the hospital on the way going or on the way back."

Darlene: "Pastor Larry (Ortman) and others are here now. Why don't you come after your appointments."

It was four-thirty by the time we got to Ardy's bedside in Kaiser Sunnyside Hospital. Ardy had expired one minute before we arrived. We stayed at Ardy's bedside with the family for two and a half hours. The love, the tender affection, the beauty of God's peace was so abundant that the nurses remarked about it. We went to dinner with the family and then we all disbursed to our own homes.

"O God, how we need your presence in times like these!" I prayed.

The peaceful acceptance and family warmth proved the great gift of God's grace. The love and peace was more rich with grace than I could ever have hoped for.

"Adele, I want you and Sam to have Ardy's service," Darlene said. "We won't have a sermon. I'd like you to give his life sketch and Sam to have some Scripture and brief remarks."

That started me writing and polishing to produce the best piece I could for this praiseworthy man. Sam went to work on his part.—all loving labor but it took time.

At Ardy's memorial service on Sunday, 1:30 P.M. there was truth, beauty, humor, reverence and deep feelings of love and admiration. Ardy was one unusually giving, unusually Christlike, unusual husband, father, and friend. Pastor Larry directed the service. He spoke kindly but briefly in his prayer and remarks. Neither Sam nor I spoke at length. But in the sharing time so many people came forward to laud Ardy for his kind and generous ways that the service stretched out to two and a half hours. We laughed and cried at the humorous and tender things that were said about this unusual man.

I prayed, "Christ Jesus, how beautiful is your character when reflected in humankind!"

The church ladies prepared a fine dinner and the visiting went on another two and a half hours. The love and joy of renewed friendships, the peace and beauty of spirit was as rich as a Christmas morning with a family of many children gathered around a green tree of God's love.

Sadness was pushed aside by "Grace that is Greater than all our woes."

"Thank you, Jesus, for the wonder we see when your grace is lived out."

No sooner had we come home from comforting Ardy's family but what we were back in the hospital to visit our dear friend, Donna Bunnell. She had hip replacement surgery. We'd been praying earnestly for her and, thanks to God, she came through fine. While we visited with Donna she told us her mother-in-law, Lana Bunnell, just died. Lana was one of the great contributors to our ministry with the wonderful life and family she afforded the work of the church. For forty years we watched this mother and family with deep admiration.

There were many ready thoughts when Roberta, the daughter, said, "Sam and Adele, we'd like you to do for Mother's service what you did for Ardy's."

Again I went to my computer and Sam to his Bible.

"Another rich life lived for you, God! Oh, the wonder of a godly family. Thank you, Lord! With a person like this, the eulogy is easy."

The day before Lana's memorial service my nephew, Preston Butcher, called. His mother and my sister Clare, died.

"We'd like for you and Sam to do the service. If that's all right, we'll come over to your house and talk about it," Preston said.

I hadn't had time to dust the furniture in a month. But that was not important.

I said, "Come." And we went into planning for another funeral service, the fourth in the month so far.

During all this activity, I broke a tooth and sat in the dentist's office for over an hour, relaxed and patient. A grace from where?

Also Sam and I each had our long-scheduled cataract surgery with its many doctor's appointments. We had twenty-twenty vision the morning after. Doctor and nurse were both surprised. "It doesn't happen often," the nurse said,

"Could this be another gift of your grace to keep us from the stress of poor vision through all our writing and reading, Lord?" I asked

One blessing was that our busy schedule left us no time for self-pity. So we never missed a beat when a precious young couple, Mike and Vanessa McQuay, whom we helped find each other and marry, called to ask if they could come for a weekend visit. Between our grandchildren, Nick and Nicola, who lived right behind us at the time, and Sam and me, we gave these loved ones a good time. One day, the two couples went on a day's hike, topped with a Cambodian dinner. The next day I enjoyed fixing the six of us a turkey dinner with mashed potatoes, gravy, fruited jello salad, marinated bean salad, cranberry sauce and blueberry pie with ice cream.

The boys ate until they groaned.

My prayers went on, "Thank you, Lord God, for your bountiful blessings!"

The third morning, Sam cooked breakfast of bacon, eggs, fried potatoes, toast with my home made strawberry jam and orange marmalade and coffee. Then we said a sweet farewell and sent these dear ones on their way, back to Victoria, B.C. They were smiling and hugging us, saying, "Thank you so much. We had a wonderful time!"

"How rich we are, dear God, in love and friendships!"

*****

Adding up all the events, there was packing and home preparation for a five day stay, a flight to Missouri and a funeral officiated; hence, four deaths, four funerals officiated; burglars' messes cleaned up, a jimmied door fixed, all outside door knobs with locks replaced, a car rented and two cars replaced; hospital calls, praying with and comforting dear, grieving relatives and friends, funerals planned with families; a tooth crowned, two cataract surgeries; entertaining out-of-town guests.

All this in less than thirty days.

"Shouldn't we be utterly spent?" I asked.

Then I answered myself and gave thanks where thanks was due.

"Yes! God, we'd be utterly spent, but for your wondrous grace that gave us the miracles of love, joy, peace, strength and endurance!"

Unbelievably, we were not even tired at the end of the month.

That in its self is a miracle!

# CHAPTER 31

# Guiding Vision

## *A. H.*

O yes, Mama was a praying woman!

Rearing eight strapping, strong-minded and downright "ornery young uns" she never went to bed before she knelt down and pleaded with God on behalf of each needy child. This, even though, after all the farm work was done, she often sat up past midnight sewing.

She made much of our clothing. She looked at a dress in a store window, went home and cut a pattern out of newspaper, tried the pattern on us piece by piece and then made the dress according to her newspaper pattern. It always fit just right.

For simple things she didn't use a pattern. I remember how I had to stand still while she tried a dress yolk on me and cut out the neckline. If I moved a bit I'd get the sharp point of the scissors in my tender skin.

I can still hear her praying for my wayward brothers. She prayed about everything. But her most earnest prayers were that her children would come to know the Living God. That the family be gathered together in heaven with not one missing, this was her dedicated goal.

And so here I was, one of the two avowed Christians out of the eight. But who could know the hearts of the others?

Mama died. The family gathered at our house after her funeral. By now we had grown to forty with spouses, children and grandchildren. With the adults arounnd the long table, it was a kind of "last supper" with memories of Mama. We paid tribute to both Mama and Daddy for their hard work and the loving labor demanded to raise the close-knit family we were and for their being the good, strong, fine Christian people we were blessed to have as parents.

So now the day was over. Everyone was gone. My husband and young son, Randy, were sitting on the divan in our living room with me in the middle. I think they wanted to console me, but a baseball game was on TV. Of course that caught their attention. This was fine with me. My mind was a long way off, meditating, as I sat in my pool of grief.

Then the vision came.

It came, a large chandelier-type crown of sparkling, burnished gold, beautifully and intricately crafted with spearlike candles in the form of angels. Their wings opened just enough to let me see their exquisite, gossamer beauty. It was as clear and real as though a fine artist and goldsmith had collaborated together to fashion it. Down from heaven it came. I saw it being lowered from the ceiling.

I froze in awe.

"This is your mother's faith," a voice spoke into my mind with resonant tones. "It is her crown of glory and her prayers of faith for her children."

The crown moved toward and over me. There it stopped, settling inches above my head. I could see it clearly. It hung over my head as real as the chandelier hung over my dining room table.

"It is now yours to fulfill. The angels of the crown will affect your work."

These words completed the vision.

Secretly, oh so secretly, I kept them in my heart and pondered them as I dedicated myself to the assigned task. Gladly I took up Mama's task of loving concern and earnest prayer for each of her children, my siblings.

Without ceasing, in prayer and in sharing God's desire to bless each one, I continued in faith, trusting the angels to do their work.

With deep gratitude, I watched it happen. One by one, in miraculous ways, six of the eight lusty kids, grown into strong, moral charactered adults, came to faith in The One Who Is The Door to that Great Gathering Place where Mama awaits us.

Only two are left. My "little sister," Anita, now 78 and I, 85, will be following them in the not-too-distant future.

Sam and I were privileged to assist the family in each memorial service of our parents and six siblings. Anita tells us Sam and I don't get to die yet. We still have to have her and her husband Del's services when they go.

Taking up Mama's cause has been one of the greatest privileges of my life. Through it all, remembering Mama's crown of faith, I've looked up and said, "How are we doing, Mama?"

I know she's pleased.

# CHAPTER 32

# His Name Is Jon

## *A. H.*

When Sam and I retired, our sole income, other than two small social security checks, was from a few rental properties we worked ever so hard to acquire, maintain, and sell on contract. Always wanting to live at the beach, we sold our home in Portland, Oregon and moved to a lovely, big house right on the ocean front, which we were able to buy on contract. Excited at last to be able to retire fully, we moved to Lincoln City, Oregon.

Hardly had we time to taste our freedom when the recession of the early '80s hit. People lost their jobs and moved out of the area by droves. Three of our buyers just walked away leaving us with empty houses. We had to make payments on the underlying mortgages whether there was income from the properties or not. We put them back on the market with realtors. But nobody was buying.

I hustled every idea that came to mind. Doing everything I knew short of giving the properties away. After all, they were our daily bread not just for a month or a year, but for the rest of our lives.

Nights I lay awake worrying over the fact that payments were stacking up and our small savings was dwindling.

What a traumatic time it was!

Finally we decided the only way we could keep from losing everything was to pack up a bachelor's kit and go live in each house, one after the other, clean, repair, paint and stay until we could rent it out. This meant we'd have to move back to Portland and leave our beloved beach house. We were still making payments on it so we'd have to rent it out, too.

We put out a signs and advertised. Weeks went by. No one showed up except groups of Hippies and people who wanted to rent for a third of its value.

Only a woman who has rented out her own home with all its personal and intimate belongings could understand my anguish.

How could we find renters we could trust to take care of our things? We couldn't afford to move and store them. In that depressed economy who would pay adequate rent and keep the property up, too?

Day and night I worried and prayed. I don't know which I did more, worry or pray. But I did both with vigor. Sam and I did a lot of fretting and no little amount of depressed grumbling which too often turned into arguing.

One particular night, again not being able to sleep, I got up in the wee hours. In slippered feet, I dragged myself down to the living room. There I sat looking out the window that stretched across the width of the house. The full moon shining on the ripples of a calm ocean made a silver path to my door.

How I hurt to think of giving up this hallowed spot. And to a stranger yet! In my anguish I cried, "Oh, God! Please send an angel to help us!"

As that sentence flew from my mind, an inaudible voice said, "I have sent an angel to help you."

Hmm, could that be so? I wondered. I thought I felt a presence standing behind my right shoulder. Am I imagining things?

"Test the voice," came to my mind.

"If you really have sent someone to help us," I said, "tell me his name."

"His name is Jon." These words came back as clear as day.

"Jon, J-O-N?" I asked in sceptical disappointment, for I could see the letters as well as hear them.

"That's not a Bible name. It should be John, J-O-H-N." I spelled it out clearly for any one who might be listening.

Was this God? I thought.

"His name is Jon."

Again I could see the letters as well as hear them, repeated in the same flat tone.

I felt fretful.

I said in a sceptical tone, "Jon is a modern name. If you, God, were going to send an angel to help us it would be 'J-o-h-n,' a Bible name."

"His name is Jon." There it came again.

Well, I thought, I'm so beside myself with worry I've cooked this all up.

And I dragged myself back upstairs to bed, disheartened, grumbling and unbelieving.

That weekend the door bell rang. Out the door window I saw a tall, pleasant-looking, sandy-haired man. When I opened the door and faced him, he asked about our rental sign tacked to the garage. I invited him in and showed him throughout the house: three large bedrooms and bath upstairs, one bedroom and half-bath down, big living and dining room across the front of the house with two huge windows and a big sliding glass door out of which the ocean made our front yard stretch to infinity. Every room, even the large kitchen, had a good ocean view.

He said he liked it.

Of course you do, I thought, I knew you would. Who wouldn't? But...

He said his wife would like it.

Of course she would! But...

He said they were thinking about buying property there but before they did he'd give his family a treat and let them live in a beach-front house for a year or so.

"Can't afford to buy right now with the interest rate so high." (It was at 25%.)

I told him what the rent was: first and last months, security deposit, cleaning fee. Did they have a pet? Yes. Another hundred dollars, pet fee.

He asked if I'd take a check. I said I would. He seemed honest and something about him made me want to trust him. I still had the house if his check bounced.

He added up the charges, wrote the check and handed it to me.

My heart nearly stopped. There was his signature, "Jon Wright," THE RIGHT J-O-N!

And of course, angels' checks don't bounce.

# CHAPTER 33

# Joshua's Story

## *A. H.*

It was 9:30, Friday night, September 3, 1999, when I heard my daughter Marydith's anguished wail over the telephone, "Mama, Joshua was killed in an accident. I can't stand it! I can't stand it! Can you come?"

"Yes, Honey, I'll come right away," I assured her.

That was the beginning of a nightmare we wanted to be awakened from.

Joshua was driving a BMW at the time of the accident. The car he hit head-on was a Ford Explorer which contained a couple and their three children. A young couple on vacation was in a third vehicle, a sedan, which was pulling a travel trailer. The sedan crashed into the Explorer, leaving tire marks that arched across the side of the Explorer. All the cars were totaled. No one in the other two vehicles was injured except one child received a small bruise on his forehead.

No one else was injured; Joshua was killed.

Joshua, our twenty-five-year-old darling, tall, handsome, big-warm-hugger, full of humor, how could he be taken from us? How could we live without him?

And, God knows, it was too much!

Marydith had already lost a son. Eric drowned when he was twenty-two months old. His father drowned ten years later. Joshua had been in an accident a week earlier that required twenty-six stitches in his back and totaled a car.

Now he was dead.

To add to Marydith's woes, for several years she had been suffering from chronic fatigue syndrome. How much more should one person take? How much more did God require of her?

Of course we ask the question, what have we done, as parents and grandparents, to deserve all these catastrophes? We strive to be faithful servants, as Marydith does. We love God. We trust him with all we have.

I hurried to put a few things in an overnight bag and within ten minutes I was ready to go. It would take three hours to get from our home in Portland, Oregon to Sisters, Oregon where Marydith lives. All the way over the mountains, for the full three hours, a refrain was repeating near my left ear. It said, "I will sing of the mercies of the Lord forever. I will sing. I will sing." I didn't pay any attention to it. It surely didn't come from my own thinking. At that time I was not in the mood to sing and I couldn't see a mercy of the Lord in this dreadful tragedy.

When Nick, another of my grandsons who was driving for me, and I arrived at my daughter's home she was sitting on the sofa in utter grief. Crushed by sorrow, she cried, "It's too much, Mama. It's too much. I can't bear it. It's too much!"

"Darling," I said, beating back my own need to wail, "Yes, it's too much. But God's grace is sufficient. He said it would be. Either it is or it isn't. If it isn't then we can't trust him. But I'm a believer. I believe there is a mercy of God for us and "a balm in Gilead for our wounded souls."

The refrain was still coming into my left ear, "I will sing of the mercies of the Lord forever. I will sing. I will sing." However, I still didn't feel it was coming from within me.

We sat up all night and wept and moaned and hugged and hoped for comfort. But no comfort came to us from words. There are no words in the human language for grief such as this.

The next day Marydith said, "I need to tell my good friend, Camille, about Joshua. She loved him so much, and I don't want her to hear it from someone else. I need to go to the river where she's gone for the Labor Day weekend."

I said, "Go. I'll stay here and wait for the others to come."

While I was alone, I sat in a little old-fashioned rocking chair thinking and praying.

"Jesus," I said, "I know you are here, right beside me. You said you would be and I believe you. Please talk to me."

This gentle voice came quietly into my left ear, "I've been singing to you all night. You will see the mercy of the Lord even in this. And you will sing. In time, Marydith will sing. She will sing, sing, sing."

"How can that be?" I asked.

Then he proceeded to show me his mercies as I sat, listening.

I thought about the young family. How would I feel if the mother, father or the children had died in the accident? Or, if the young couple were dead?

"Small comfort in the face of the grief you are bearing?"

"Oh, No! A big mercy!"

"How would you feel if Joshua had survived with head injuries that caused abnormal brain function? Or that put him in a wheelchair for life? Would you choose that?"

"No! No! Oh, no!"

"A mercy?"

"Yes, yes indeed."

"Lord, you saved everyone else. Why not Joshua?"

"This was Joshua's time to go to another place to learn, work and serve." These were the very words I heard in my mind.

Then I felt a strong sense of Joshua's presence in the room. So I asked, "Joshua, do you have to go someplace?"

I heard my grandson's voice say, "Yes. But I'm going later. I'm going to hang around these guys for a while."

I sensed Jesus had given him the privilege to stay and comfort us: his mother, brother, grandparents, and all his other relatives and friends for whom he cared so much. *

Quietly I thanked God for the mercies he had just revealed to me. Although I was not relieved of my pain, I knew "there is a balm in Gilead" and there is a comforting Saviour who walks with us and talks with us. He said, "My sheep know my voice."

As the song writer said, "I have walked alone with Jesus in a fellowship divine…I have seen him. I have known him. And he deigns to walk with me. And the glory of his presence shall be mine eternally."

Was I comforted that day sitting in Marydith's house?

By faith, I could say through my tears, "God is good. His mercies endure forever. And yes, I believe—in time we will sing again. We will sing."

*****

My experience of talking with Joshua may not seem credible to many believers. There was a time when I would have questioned someone who claimed to have had conversation with a deceased relative. However, in the past fifty years I've known of many others. These were Christians who told me that their deceased loved ones came to them with comforting words.

And besides, I've finally reckoned with the fact that Jesus has the right and the power to do whatever he chooses, regardless of my dogmatic beliefs.

That was no little concession for me to make.

P. S. Less than a year after Marydith's great loss, God did give her a song. She called me one day and said, "Mama, I have two grandbabies. Last night Jill and Brett got identical twin boys and I was able to be there for the birthing."

Jesus said Marydith would sing, sing, sing! Although she still weeps, she also sings.

# CHAPTER 34

# A Little Angel?

## *A. H.*

For several years before this incident, I had studied and drilled myself in the teachings of E. Stanley Jones, the world missionary who was a personal friend of Mahatma Gandhi. At this time, I was especifically practicing his instructions, "listen, learn, obey" given in my favorite book, *Abundant Living.* Jones quotes Jesus saying, "My sheep know my voice and they follow me." He adds, the only way to abundant life is to train your mind to hear God's voice as he speaks into your heart. "Listen, learn, obey, that's the formula to abundant life."

Day after day I practiced listening to the still small voice in my heart. If what I felt or heard was true, kind, and good, I could know it was from God, Jones said. Jones directed me to the Bible's fifteenth chapter of St. John. This proved to be my gold mine, the richest strike of my life. In John 15:1-17 Jesus says, "I am the vine and you're the branch, abide in me and I'll abide in you and my father will prune you. But you'll bear much fruit." (my translation)

So, "Listen, Learn, Obey," became my obsession.

This particular morning I had three letters in the upper pocket of my husband's red flannel shirt which I was wearing. One letter was from my mother. She was telling me that Daddy had several light strokes after the big one he recovered from and that she hoped we could come home to have Christmas with the family.

"This may be the last Christmas we can all be together," she wrote.

Enclosed with her letter were two others; one from my sister, Anita, who then lived in Phoenix, Arizona, saying she and her family planned to be at Mama's house for Christmas. The other was from my brother Herb, who lived in Brazil. He was coming home for the first time in many years.

"All the other children will be here, I hope you and your family can come, too." Mama wrote.

Oh! how I wanted to go!

But it was in the early 1950s. We were poor young pastors of that small, struggling church. There was barely enough in our budget for food and the necessary clothing, let alone gas for a four-thousand mile round trip from Muskogee, Oklahoma to Portland, Oregon. I talked to Sam. He said he didn't see how we could possibly make it.

Jesus says "If you live in me you can ask anything in my name and my Father will give it to you" (John 15:16). I would tell my yearning desire to God.

As I often did, to have a quiet place to pray, I went into the bathroom and locked the door. There I got on my knees. With forehead touching the floor, I implored God to make a way for me and my family to go home to Portland, Oregon for Christmas.

A faint knock sounded on the door. I knew it was our two-year-old-son, Randy. I began to say, "Honey, Mama's praying. Will you go play now?"

Before I could speak I heard that inner voice say, "It's an angel. Let it in."

Listening, and having learned, I obeyed.

Opening the door, I said, "Honey, come in."

"Tell it to bless you," the voice said.

"Honey, lay your hands on Mama's head and pray for her," I said.

Our darling did and his prayer was,

"Thank you, Jesus, for this food.

Bless all the children in the world."

Now I had the choice of feeling foolish, as though he was blessing headcheese by praying a blessing on "this food." Or, I could believe God sent him to bless my desire to go home for Christmas. Knowing a prayer is a prayer and God can unscramble it, I chose the latter. I rose feeling I had obeyed.

When I got up, there were my three letters, fallen out of my pocket, lying on the floor. Across them was an old billfold that Randy had been playing with. The billfold straddled all three of my letters. That same voice which instructed me to let the angel in said, "There, Child, is your need and my supply. Go in peace."

I went in peace—and in GREAT JOY!

I started laundering and laying aside articles of clothing in preparation for our trip. Each person had a neat pile on top of his or her dresser. I did the chores needed to close up the house for two weeks. My work was light—with joyous praise!

Behold! Just a few days before we were to leave, money came in the mail: from a person who had never sent us money before; car insurance from a minor accident paid off; our congregation decided to take up a love offering for us.

One little Sunday school boy told me, "I emptied my piggy bank and gave it to you so you can go home for Christmas."

We had dollars enough to go "home for Christmas!"

With a couple paper boxes for suitcases, I was packed and ready.

I don't know why I use suitcases now. Of course, they look better. But paper boxes are so cheap, light and handy.

# CHAPTER 35

# Saved from a Wheelchair

## *A. H.*

I was just months away from being pushed around in a wheelchair. In fact, at one time I was pushed around in a wheel chair.

My daughter wanted me to go with her and her fourteen-year-old son to Disney Land. "Mama," she pleaded, "this is probably the last time Joshua will want to take a trip with us. Please come."

I couldn't see myself walking around in Disney Land. I could hardly walk a few blocks without intense pain in my hips. It was just that winter I walked two and a half blocks to our church where I was to lead a small "Growth Group" meeting. I went to the church early to make preparation. When I got there the side door was locked. It was another block around the building to the other door. I realized it might be open. But I was in so much pain I just sat down on the cold concrete step and cried, "Dear Lord Jesus, I can't walk another step. Please help me."

After nearly freezing my bottom on the ice cold step and chilling the rest of me in the bitter wind, I thought, I'm going to take pneumonia. I'd better try to make it around the building. Maybe that door is unlocked. I struggled up and put one aching foot in front of the other until I reached the other door—Locked!

"Oh, God help me!" I cried.

The church custodian lived just across the parking lot. But I'd have to walk that block and another half block around his house to get to his door. I calculated every step. I can't make it, I thought.

"God, you'll have to send an angel to help me," I prayed. Then I stood and waited for God's answer.

Soon one of our Sunday school boys came whizzing through the parking lot on his bicycle. "Hi, Mrs. Hooker!" he shouted.

"Hey! wait Honey, please come back," I called after him. He came.

"Will you go over to the custodian's house there and ask him to come unlock the church door for me?"

"Sure!" he said and whizzed away.

In minutes the door was unlocked and I was able to prepare for our meeting.

That was twenty-seven years ago. But the incident and the pain are still as vivid in my mind as they were that bitter, cold, dark, discouraging night. I knew I was on my way to the greater pain of hip replacement or a wheel chair.

Yes, I did go to Disney Land with my daughter and grandson. And yes, I did end up in a wheelchair.

For a short while I walked around the grounds with the two of them. Then I spotted a nice bench in an area where I could see much of the fun that was going on.

"You kids go play," I said, "I'll sit here and join you again a little later."

"Oh Mama!" Marydith cried, "How can I be so thoughtless. I'm getting you a wheel chair."

With that she sped off and came back running with that blue and silver rolling thing that I despised. From then on she pushed me up to a gate, got in line and when it was her turn, she led me into the fun ride. We had a jolly good time. But for me it was dark-clouded with what that wheel chair portended.

Back home, at our church, one of the "Growth Group" members

asked me if Sam and I would host another group trip to the Holy Lands. "You did it before," Sandy said, "this time Davie and I want to go along."

"Yes, we did," I told her, "but not any more. All that walking is too much for me now."

"Sandy," I whined, "I'd love to get another group together and have you and Davie in it. It would be so much fun to travel with you. But I just can't. I can hardly walk two blocks now. The arthritis in my hips is getting worse all the time." I told her about my wheelchair ride at Disney Land and my "nearly not making the walk" around the church building.

"Oh! you won't need to walk much. Davie and I will push you in a wheelchair and we'd love to do it!"

"Honey, you know I'd love to go. But that would be a bummer for everyone."

The next Sunday evening at our church service, I couldn't believe what I saw and heard. This exceedingly shy girl got up in front of the whole congregation and said, "I'd like to ask you all to pray for Sister Hooker. She is suffering badly with arthritis in her hips. Davie and I want her and Pastor Sam to take us on a tour with them to the Holy Lands. She says she'd love to but she can't walk that much. Please pray she'll be healed."

I don't remember that anyone came up to me and specifically said they were praying for me. Maybe one or two did. But it wasn't many weeks until I could walk pretty well. I did get a group together and we surely did take Sandy and David Harrison with us to the Holy Lands. We had an exciting and memorable excursion.

Now, twenty years later, at the time of this writing, I'm eighty-two years old. I take no medication whatsoever. And each morning Sam and I walk in the Clackamas Town Center Mall. I like to fast-walk and I walk an extra round from what Sam does. I cover about two and a half to three miles. I have no pain in my hips or back. I can run fast, too!

Often I tell God, "I'm skipping and dancing and running, and I'd turn somersaults too if I could, in praise of You. You have done great things for me and I am glad, glad, glad!"

# CHAPTER 36

# Listen, Learn, Obey

## *A. H.*

Often I've mentioned Dr. E. Stanley Jones, the world missionary and personal friend with Mahatma Gandhi. He taught me the important elements of having a friendship with Jesus.

God, our heavenly Father, Jones said, wants a relationship with his children. God gave us himself in the flesh and blood of Jesus, so we could envision him and have a personal friendship with him. We need to learn how to commune with Jesus. The way is to listen to that still, small voice within us.

Jones told me to let Jesus use my mind in the same way I let others commune with me through words that become thoughts.

"Listen to God. Learn to hear his messages and obey the voice of love and truth. This is the formula for Abundant Living," Jones told me.

For over fifty years now, I have practiced that. And I'm thrilled to feel this wonderful peace and joy I have when I hold conversation with God in Jesus.

One night I was praying for a very dear friend. He was having financial difficulty. He lost his job due to being honest. I felt God talked to me, giving me instructions as to what God wanted me to do for him, for God.

I listened.

I feel I have learned to know God's voice.

I obeyed.

The outcome of it was these letters.

Dear David, (name changed)

It's four o'clock in the morning and I've been praying for you. In my head I heard these words, "Send David $100."

I said, "I will God, if that's you talking to me."

He said, "I want you to."

Now you have to know, I have lots of conversations with God. And years ago I made a solemn commitment by saying to God, (because he did for me something I struggled long to do and couldn't) "I'll never say 'No' to you again."

I said, "OK, I'll do it first thing in the morning."

He said, "Do it now."

I said, "You want me to do it now? Why?"

He said, "That he'll better know I love him and I care."

Another commitment I made to God is that I promised to "Listen, Learn and Obey." And I would obey immediately if I was convinced it was God talking to my mind—instead of my own imaginings.

And you know, David, that I'm a woman of integrity. Of all things, I won't lie to myself or to God.

So here you are—my check. Don't thank me, thank God!

But please remember, I love you, too.

Your friend who cares so much for you and prays a lot for you, too.

Adele

I wrote out the check, addressed the envelope, put the check in it. I made a copy of the letter before I sealed it. The feeling that came over me was one of pure joy. I went back to bed smiling.

I know we can't put God in debt to us, so it's not a sacrifice to obey him. He always pays us back, usually with interest—"ten, twenty and a hundred fold," the Bible tells us. So, I didn't do a great thing by sending $100. The great thing I did was to "Listen, (having learned) and Obey."

For me, that's always fun. In fact, I think God's more fun than anyone I've ever known. We have a lot of fun together!

And why shouldn't God be fun? He made it in the first place. So, it must come from him.

Here is the reply I got from my letter and check.

> Hi, Adele,
>
> Sorry it took me so long to email you but I lost your address and had to get it again. I suppose if I had sent you a letter it would have arrived sooner.
>
> Anyway, I wanted to thank you for the check even though you said it was from God, not you.
>
> I know why he said to send it. At the time I was standing on my front porch trying to decide if I would pay the electric bill or buy food. I called into the house to Jerrid and said, "We can have electricity or food. We don't have money for both. Which do you want?"
>
> Just then the mailman handed me your letter. Weird, huh?
>
> Well, thanks again. The money could not have come at a better time.
>
> Love,
> David

The third part of this story is that just a few days after I sent the $100 check, I got $108 in the mail. I sure wasn't expecting it! The pay back figured out at 35% interest.

It's true; you can't put God in debt to you. So lighten up! Listen. Learn. Obey. It really is fun!

Reading this again I asked myself why I put it in the book. One reason is not to make myself look good! In fact, I almost left it out for that reason—it might make me look good and I'm not that good. I'm no better than you! I've just been fortunate enough to learn one of life's most precious and fun secrets. This gift of knowledge from E. Stanley Jones has blessed my life for over fifty years.

So why include the incident?

To tell others with practice they too can hear God speak to them. And to say it's the most joyful way to live—"Abundant Living," E. Stanley Jones called it and so it is! So it is!

At the beginning of my "Abundant Living" lessons I said, "But how will I know it's you speaking to me, God"

His answer came immediately, "I am Goodness, Love, and Truth. I will never prostitute my character."

Have I ever remembered that!

If you want to live in greater peace and joy, here's the formula.

1. Train yourself to listen for God's still, small voice inside your heart.
2. Learn to recognize God's voice.
3. Identify it by God's characteristics: peace, goodness, love, joy and truth.
4. Quietness helps. Meditation is necessary!
5. Be willing to obey God.
6. Obey—just do it if it's loving and kind.
7. Practice. Practice. Practice.
8. Read the Bible to learn more about this life enhancing subject.

Like anything else, learning takes time and practice. But Oh! It's a gold strike when you do learn it—and miracles follow. Yes, indeed they do! Just ask David.

# CHAPTER 37

# And Then There Was Indy

## *A. H.*

There are people who relate to their pets with love similar to what they would toward a child. "She's my baby," a lady said to me when I admired her spunky, little, black and white Chihuahua.

"We've got three dogs, they're our kids," one man said to Sam and me.

Many people consider this ridiculous. I remember the strong, critical feeling I had as a young person when I saw a well-dressed, older woman in a fancy car, hugging a little pomeranian dog. How ludicrous! I thought, why doesn't she give that love and attention to a needy child!

But years later when our children were grown and gone from home, I understood. I surely did not want to start over rearing children!

Then I was given a smart, little, fawn colored Chihuahua. The more this little being's personality shone through, the more my husband and I enjoyed her funny antics. She filled our days with laughter and the warmth of her love. We became attached to her, as she depended on us. After a while she did seem like our baby. She even slept under the covers with us.

In fact, toward her ending days, when she was sick with cancer, I wrapped her in a baby blanket and took her to church with me. I wouldn't leave this sick little-one home for hours alone.

So we gained understanding and compassion from the experience of having a beloved pet for thirteen years. Now that knowledge would transfer when we took care of our grandson's cat named Indy.

Indy was Brett's buddy. We were keeping him because Brett was in a center for drugs and alcohol rehabilitation. Indy had many sweet ways. Often I'd tell Sam to look at Indy's peaceful expression as he slept with his white paws curled up under his pumpkin colored chin. When he wanted something he'd come up to where I was sitting, stand on his hind legs and, reaching up as high as he could, with a gentle paw he'd tap my upper arm. I thought this was brilliant! If I was standing, he'd look up at me patiently and softly meow. He was a "gentleman," a fourteen-year-old-wise-one.

We cared for Indy with consideration. I bought him the best. Soon "people-tuna" was the only kind he'd eat. He was worth it.

"Why don't you give him the pet tuna and make him like it?" Sam said. "If he's hungry enough he'll eat it."

"Why should we do that to him in his old age?" I answered. "People tuna doesn't cost that much more and besides I only put a small amount on his dry food."

I didn't voice it but I reasoned to myself, I not only love him but I'm old, too, and I feel for his feelings. How do I want others to treat me when I'm dependent on them? Secretly, I held to this rationale and treated Indy accordingly.

But now Indy was very time consuming, constantly wanting out and in, out and in. It seemed like he found a new game. Or maybe he was so old he forgot he had just been out a few minutes ago. Maybe he was having kidney problems. I kept accommodating him. Occasionally he soiled the rug with vomiting and also with dirt and debris he dragged in on his sagging belly. These were no small annoyances to both Sam and me.

Yes, Indy was a lover. But some times we'd ask each other, "How long do we have to endure the burden of a cat?"

When Sam and I retired we said we'd have no more pets. My mind sometimes scolded me, I thought you weren't going to start all over again with pets.

Indy increased his vomiting. The dirt, leaves and other stuff he dragged into the house kept the rugs in need of vacuuming. His coat was constantly matting. It was drab and greasy in spite of the fact that I brushed him daily. He shed excessively. Everywhere, in every room of the house, there was not only the normal cat hair, but large, orange tufts.

In spite of everything, because he was old and away from his original family, we took pity on him and gave him the run of the house and yard.

Sometimes, when the poor little fellow got real sick, I hoped he'd lie under a bush and let himself go to cat heaven. (There's surely such a place. Anyway, it helped me to imagine it.) But he'd always recover enough to come back.

We were already doing much for our grandson to help him get off drugs and onto a stable life. Sometimes I thought, Isn't it enough? Do we owe him the strain and stress of caring for this burdensome cat? Then I'd shame myself for criticizing this poor little being who couldn't help himself. Why am I not more self-giving? I'd ask.

To put a pet down, for most of us is not an easy matter. When do we take a life God created? That's just one question. Many other thoughts entered in. How would my grandson feel if he lost his good friend? They were together for fourteen years. They had fun together. Brett and his then-wife had a circus of three cats. They made for an entertaining evening. Indy was Brett's comfort through his divorce. The two traveled together. They were inseparable. Brett dearly loved him, calling Indy "my little man." Everywhere Brett moved, Indy moved with him. When Brett flew from Oregon to Ottawa, Canada, Indy flew, too.

Now should I put added grief on Brett when he was struggling fiercely in this tough rehab program?

Decision making became ensnarled with beliefs, and emotions. My mind boiled in its quandary. How much should I require of myself? How much more should I give? Indy was an eighty-five percent burden. Sam was good about cleaning up Indy's vomit, mostly relieving me of the unpleasant work. How about Sam's comfort? He wondered at my willingness to have the rugs messed but he didn't criticize me. I appreciated that.

Then our son and daughter-in-law, Grant and Pam, visited us from Ottawa, Canada where Indy had been with them at a time past. Pam couldn't get over the condition of Indy: his pitiful looks, his dragging stomach, his greasy hair. She wanted to give him a bath. I felt the poor little creature should not be subject to such trauma. My son said he'd help us if we wanted to "put him down." The euphemism I used was to "let him go see Jesus."

I didn't really believe that. However I did reason, How do we know about the great expanses. How do we know what God has out there for every living thing? Could energy die? Sure, a flame can be snuffed out, but does that mean the spirit of a life goes out, too? Doesn't the energy of flame go on in smoke?

All this and more kept me from making a decision. My son felt it was no big deal. "Just see how bad off the cat is and reckon with the big burden he is to you," Grant advised.

We all know Indy is not well. But how sick is he?

Grant didn't know the anguished thoughts I was having. It was a big deal to me.

Here were the entanglements that kept me in this quandary.

I loved Brett and didn't want to depress him further right at that time. Brett loved Indy dearly.

For fourteen years Indy was Brett's buddy.

Indy was still somewhat healthy.

I loved Indy. He still had cute ways. But, yes, he was very burdensome.

Brett and Brett's mother loved Indy. Would they hold it against me if he were put down?

Is it a valid idea that nothing ends? Could it be that spirit lives on forever? If so, how?

None of us know for sure.

Is God in all things and all things in God? God is Good and is all good a part of God? Indy is good. So what would happen to the good that is in Indy?

I couldn't share my thoughts with anyone They'd have thought me senile for sure.

Another set of reasonings came to mind.

Could the fact that Grant and Pam were here right then be providential?

Grant offered to go with Sam to take Indy to the humane society. That would keep me from having to go with Sam.

This convenient opportunity would not last but for a few days. A decision needed to be made.

The family said since the cat was in my care, I was responsible to make the decision.

The stress of indecision was getting to me. Finally I thought to pray.

How come I didn't pray sooner?

I said this prayer,

"God, you know Indy is old and he often vomits on our carpet.

Also he makes a mess by dragging in dirt and losing hair tufts on the rug and on our bed.

I don't want to deny this dear little entity the comfort of home as long as he is alive.

Help me to know what to do."

Thought came, "Put out a fleece."

Okay, I will.

I will call Marydith and tell her I don't want to keep Indy and see what advice she has to offer. If a positive plan comes from her, I'll accept it. If not, I'll consider the other way out.

Several times I phoned but got no answer.

Then I said, "Jesus, please help me know what to do."

As quick as those words left my mind, these words entered, "Let the little one come to me."

Oh, I loved it! My heart leaped! I had often said jokingly, "Indy is old and although I love him, I wish he would go see Jesus." And now I felt free to send this little spirit into God's care. Maybe in God's great expanse, there is a place for cats. Peace, like a gentle, warm, shower washed over me. Without giving details, I told Sam to do whatever he saw fit while Pam and I took a two day trip to see our daughter in Sisters, Oregon.

When we returned home there was a small, new grave in our garden with a pretty stone to mark it.

This was my very small, personal miracle: Peace came from God with these words, "Let the little one come to me."

I am filled with gratitude.

# CHAPTER 38

# The Road Less Traveled

## *A. H.*

The other day I was visiting with my younger sister Anita and her daughter Kim. I don't know how the subject came up, but Anita said to Kim, "Adele was always different."

At the time I didn't question why she said that. But later, as I thought on it, a significant fact came to mind. As M. Scott Peck said, "I took the road less traveled by. And that made all the difference."

And yes, that was the same for me. "I took the road less traveled by and that made all the difference."

Many times I've looked back and pondered the number of incidents that were turning points in my life—times when I stood at the crossroads. Here is one of those significant moments. It made all the difference in my life. And perhaps it did make me seem different from the rest of my siblings.

\*\*\*\*\*\*

One evening when I was twelve years old my sister Emily and her husband Otto took me to church. There, in an evangelistic meeting, was a young preacher with a guitar. No doubt he preached a meaningful sermon and it probably had something to do with what followed. But what impressed me was when, with guitar in hand, he walked back and forth across the platform, strumming and singing. These are his words I will long remember.

> "When I've gone the last mile of the way,
> I shall rest at the close of the day.
> And I know there are joys that await me
> When I've gone the last mile of the way.

Then I was convinced from previous hellfire preaching that there was not only joys that awaited me but also torment if I was not good. I had already made up my mind many months earlier that I was not going to hell. The situation for that decision was an impressive and memorable one. It had much to do with my very clean and disciplined mother.

Every Saturday we kids had to do a thorough job of house cleaning. One big and dreaded task was to scrub and wax the linoleum floors of our living and dining rooms. No liquid and self-polishing wax for us.

Oh, no! It was that old-time-paste-wax that came in a shiny, round, tin can. My big sister, Clare, crawling on her hands and knees and with a small rag spread the wax on the scrubbed and dried floor—very thin and even. A brief time allowed the wax to dry. Then, with big, soft rags, we little kids got down and rubbed, rubbed, rubbed the floors until they shone. We couldn't cheat and skip a patch. That was obvious. The floor on that spot was dull. It was easy to spot these areas against the shiny ones. We were soundly scolded and sent back to do the job right.

I was littlest of the three siblings, so I got the tight places where the others didn't want to work. One of those places was behind our big, pot bellied, wood, heating stove. It stood a couple feet from the wall and in the winter time it was fired up to red-hot.

Can you see a little nine-year-old, blond girl with a rag almost as big as she was, fretting and crying behind a big, red-hot stove, rubbing, rubbing, rubbing the floor until it shone? That was me.

Oh, how I hated it! How hot it was. How miserable I was. If hell is as hot as this I'm not going there. That was the solemn vow I made to myself. From then on I tried my best to be good and to avoid anything that would make God mad at me. I didn't want him to throw me into hell at the end of my life.

I know! I know! It was a childish idea, you say. But children do get strong, impressive ideas.

Well, the tall, young, black-curly-haired preacher-man with his guitar sang about a place of joys that await us. That's where I intended to go. But I knew there was also a place of torment awaiting at the last mile of the way. My sister, Emily may have noticed my uneasiness. She leaned over and asked, "Adele, do you want to go to the altar and give your heart to Jesus?"

—and make sure you don't go to hell, my mind added.

I nodded a quick yes and Emily and I walked down the middle aisle of the sanctuary. We both knelt at the altar in front of the congregation. Emily said a prayer that I repeated. With that I was free. What a relief! There'd be no hell for me at the last mile of the way!

Right then I took "the road less traveled"—by most of the other kids in my family. They were out to have fun in a worldly way. I stayed by my commitment and took the more somber path.

This road took me to Pacific Bible College where I'd prepare to be a missionary. Here I met a young ministerial student whom I married and joined in pastoral ministry. Now I'm retired but I haven't quit serving in this "different" way.

And oh, God was good to me! I loved the pastoral ministry! I had a passion for helping people find Jesus and to develop an intimate relationship with him. It was an honor for me to be allowed into people's hurting hearts. Praying with them, seeking God's healing and his guidance, always brought us closer to each other and closer to God. It has been my deepest desire—to walk with God and to help others find the joy of doing so.

Now I have a strong hunch God was in all my decisions. I think he was there at every crossroad, guiding me to "take the road less traveled by." And yes, miraculously, "that made all the difference."

# CHAPTER 39

# Two Bissett-Family Miracles

## *Ruth Bissett*

### FIRST MIRACLE
### A Herd of Horses Named Charley?

"That looks like our grandson, Robert," I said to my husband Earl as we approached the tent where the evening service of our church youth camp was being held. The boy was sitting with his leg up, a staff member on either side and a pair of crutches handy.

That couldn't be our Robert, I thought, our Robert is vigorous and athletic, no crutches for him!

The closer we got the more I had to admit, "It's Robert!"

"Honey, what happened?" I asked in fright.

"I was just in line at the cafeteria when all of a sudden my leg hurt so bad they had to help me hobble to a bench. My leg's hard and really hurts. But I don't want to go home!" came the response from a pretty courageous young man in his early teens.

Sure enough the calf of Robert's leg was like stone. My grandmotherly instinct kicked in fast. "Wait here, I'm going for help." I called friends in the medical field for advice. They advised me to take him to the hospital emergency room immediately. This was the camp nurse's assessment at the beginning, but I wanted another opinion.

I was glad we had come in our motor home with the thought of staying the night at camp. This allowed Robert to lie down. With his grandfather in the co-pilot's seat, off we went on the curvy road, winding through the mountain. My heart was racing, I wanted to hurry but I had to keep my speed down for safety. All the while I kept praying, "God help us! God help us!"

"Are you okay, Honey?" I kept asking Robert. Each time a painful sigh came back.

"Yeah."

The motor home had lumbered on for about six miles when all of a sudden a shout came from the back, "Grandma! Grandma! It quit hurting! My leg doesn't hurt any more!"

I looked in the rear view mirror and saw a bright, happy boy jumping up and down, eager to get out of the motor home. When I found a place to pull off the highway and open the door, Robert bounded out, jumped up and down, ran up the highway in shocked glee. I called him to myself and felt his leg. It was as soft as ever before.

If it was a charley horse, then all I can say is, a whole herd of charley horses galloped out as fast as they galloped in.

When we wound our way back, we learned the entire camp had been in prayer for Robert. There were loud voices in praise and thanksgiving to God for his gracious intervention that kept a reluctant boy from having to leave all the camp fun, and go home.

I added my grateful praise and will long remember the exciting answer to anxious prayers.

## SECOND MIRACLE
### Secret Prayer Request

Our son married in his early thirties. He and his wife, both with college degrees, were very motivated in their careers. For seven years, while our younger daughter and son-in-law had their three children, our son and his wife were busy in the world of big business. Though there was talk of children when the family got together, George and Mary* never indicated that they wanted to expand their family. Since they are very private people, we didn't think it appropriate to ask when they, too, were going to make us grandparents. We assumed, with their strong involvement in the corporate world, they thought it best not to have children.

One February day my husband and I were traveling in their area. I called to see if we could get together with them before we headed for home. To my surprise George said it wouldn't work because they were involved in the whole new arena.

"To you old timers," George kiddingly said, "it is known as a fertility clinics. We've been trying to conceive for five years and we're running out of options. It'll be a miracle if it happens. I'm sorry the timing won't work out for us to see you right now."

"You can know we'll be praying for that miracle!" I said. And my grandmotherly instinct kicked in hard again. I called everyone I knew to get God's people praying. I just asked my church to pray for an urgent unspoken request.

My heart pounded every time I saw a mother with a baby or young child. I thought about the heartbreak my son and daughter-in-law must have been feeling. I knew, as anyone who observed them knew, they would be wonderful parents.

By May, after it all started in February, our son called and was pretty insistent that we and our daughter's family get together on Mother's Day. I was taken aback a bit. Since they lived a distance from us, we didn't usually get together for Mother's Day. But I always treasure any time we can be together. We set a time and place for dinner.

On that Mother's Day I was given the best gift I could have received—

an ultrasound picture of our little miracle! They had waited until after the first trimester to give us the good news.

It was then we could happily reveal our secret of the unspoken prayer request. Now our spoken request was for safe delivery of this baby.

But wait, the story continues! When our grandson was born, the umbilical cord was in a knot. The nurse said it was a miracle he was born alive. Many times when this happens babies are stillborn. Now we have a two-miracle grandson!

And, are we praising God!

# CHAPTER 40

# House on Fire

## *A. H.*

Marydith saved our house!

It happened on a day when the children were all three in school. Sam and I had a ten o'clock appointment in Salem which is an hour's drive from our home in Portland. We left shortly after the children went to school. No one would be home until late afternoon.

Marydith, who was fifteen at the time, was in her English class at Franklin High School. Something was bothering her, but she didn't know what. So preoccupied was she, that she didn't know what the teacher was saying. All she knew was: she didn't want to be sitting there; she didn't want to be in school; she wanted to go home.

But how could she tell her teacher how she felt?

Of course, she wanted to go home. Lots of the kids did. Of course, she didn't want to be sitting in that class room. Lots of kids didn't. But the longer she sat the more miserable she became. Could she just get up and walk out?

No. The teacher would stop her. If she ran, the school authorities would send someone to get her. What could she do?

She was in a quandary.

Finally her irritation mounted. Anxiety cut in. She had to go home! She just had to go home.

She trembled to walk up to the teacher's desk. But she did, and said, "Mrs. Moreland, I feel I need to go home. May I go?"

"Are you sick, Marydith?" Mrs. Moreland asked.

"No. I'm not sick. I just have this strong feeling that I need to go home. I don't know why. But I feel I need to go home."

"Well, Marydith," Mrs. Moreland said, musing, "You're a good student and you've never tried to get out of class before. I think you might need to go home for some reason. I'm going to give you a hall pass and let you go home. I hope everything is all right when you get there. Here's the pass. Good luck."

Marydith walked the mile and a half to our house. She came in the door. No one was home. The empty house seemed spooky. She didn't know why she was there. Now, she thought, I'd rather be back in class. She became more and more frightened. She went into her room and locked the door.

Then she heard a noise. Was someone in the house? She sat on her bed and prayed, asking God to take care of her and "Please send Mama and Daddy home soon."

Trembling with fear, she waited and listened but heard nothing more. Carefully she opened her door to better hear any other noises. Maybe the person who was in the house left, she thought.

No more noise but—"oh, the smell—It's smoke!"

It was coming from the basement stairway. She ran down, opened the door, and the smoke whirled up out of the basement. Marydith ran into the laundry room to find the ironing board on fire. She grabbed the only thing she could get her hands on, a coke bottle and a small pitcher. She poured water on the fire but it didn't do any good. She ran upstairs and called the fire department. They came and put the fire out.

The iron cord was burnt in two and the shoe of the iron was melted.

The fireman told Marydith had she gone in earlier and poured water on the iron or cord as it was burning she would have been electrocuted. The pop she heard was the cord snapping in two. So, to her good fortune, the electricity was off.

When we got home, we called the Oregonian and a reporter came. He took a picture of Marydith and the melted iron and put a write-up in the newspaper.

Our hearty thanks to God! He moved on Marydith's thoughts and feelings to get up courage enough to ask to go home. Thanks to her kind teacher who trusted her and let her go home. Thanks to God that Marydith was afraid and didn't go down to the basement before the cord snapped. Thank to God and Marydith for saving our house and all our possessions. And thank to God, most of all, that we didn't lose our daughter in the effort.

*****

Here again is an example of E. Stanley Jones' famous three words for "Abundant Living," "Listen, Learn, Obey."

I thank God, Marydith did all three.

And I thank God he urged Marydith strongly enough to do it and then guided her in a safe manner.

# CHAPTER 41

# Now I Know He's Real

*Carolyn Goin*

I was five years old and the youngest of five siblings. Every night I sat on my parent's bed with my sister and three brothers while our mother read to us out of Egemeier's Bible Story Book.

One night after the reading I asked, "Mama, how do I know Jesus is real?"

"Pray and ask Jesus to show you that he is real," Mom answered.

So I did. When I crawled into my small bed I said, "Jesus, please show me that you are real. I want to know."

In the middle of the night I woke up and looked across the room to where my sister was sleeping. There, standing at her bedside, was a tall man in a white robe. I couldn't see his face clearly, but it glowed. Frightened, I closed my eyes tight and pulled the covers over my head. Then I thought, Maybe Jesus is showing me that he is real. So I uncovered my eyes enough to peak from under the covers. He was gone.

But I knew from then on that Jesus was real and he was trying to show it to me.

Now every time I doubt, I remember that night most vividly. And I say to him, "Jesus, I know you are real and you are taking care of me and those I love."

That incident was with me years later when, as a grown young woman, I felt desperate.

It was a warm, clear, late-summer-night in Ridgefield, Washington of 1998. Although I was alone from a divorce, I had a beautiful home on five acres of land. I had a beloved mare, Lacy. She and her foul were bedded down in a new barn. I thought I was through grieving over my broken marriage. I told myself I had everything I needed and it ought to make me happy. But I was miserable.

I sat in my hot tub looking up at the stars. My mind went back to the incident of seeing Jesus when I was five years old. I cried to God. I told him how worthless my life was and how hopeless I felt.

"God," I said, "I love you so much and it seems there is nothing I can do for you. I've let you down. All these bumps and turns in my life have left me helpless. I'm a failure."

Was that an audible voice I heard? I think so, but I'm not sure. It said, "It is not what you can do for me, but what I can do for you."

At that moment I opened my arms and my heart. I embraced the immediate presence of my Lord, Jesus Christ. I began enjoying him every day in prayer and meditation. Not only at that set time once a day, but all day long.

A new journey started.

I was contacted by a prestigious riding academy in the East. They invited me to Maryland to work and learn at their English riding club. Horses were my love and I had many trophies from riding shows. This, a new style to me, was what, for several years, I had wanted to learn. In Maryland and in New Jersey I apprenticed as a riding instructor.

After a year and a half I came west again to be the director of a large horseback riding academy in Aurora, Oregon. There, for three years I had the opportunity to influence the lives of many children and even some adults.

Sitting on a park bench one night, watching my dog run and play, I said to God, "Okay, God, I'm ready now to give back. What can I do for you?"

After that, in a mode of alertness, I waited for his answer. Often I wondered if he was saying, "Start your own business."

A year later I did just that. I opened my own riding school. Now it is the "Goin Places Riding School" by Carolyn Goin, Hunter Seat Equitation Instructor, Sherwood, Oregon.

I'm no longer a depressed, hopeless failure. God and I are in business together sharing moral integrity, faith and Jesus' love with both children and adults.

To God be the glory!

# CHAPTER 42

# I'm Alive!

## *Victor Grice*

During the Korean War, which lasted from 1950 to 1953, I was stationed in the Southern Pacific War Zone on the USS JUNO—named after Juno Alaska. We were just off the Coast of North Korea, shelling them pretty heavy.

It was a clear night with a bright moon.

At about 10 P. M. a fog bank rolled in. The fog was so thick we couldn't see twenty feet ahead. Then at 2 P. M. the fog was gone in a second. Looking around you couldn't see a patch of fog anywhere. It gave the starboard lookout clear vision. He saw the wake of North Korean torpedo boats coming straight at us. With five inch guns we shelled and sank all but one. He got away.

Two survivors we picked up out of the water.

A little Japanese boy, a US sailor, was on board with us. He grew up with his family in San Francisco and spoke Japanese. He could understand Korean since the languages are much the same.

From him we learned the Korean soldiers were fifteen years old. There were six PT boats. They were instructed not to fire their torpedos, but to ram us. It was a suicide mission. Under cover of the fog, they were to ram and sink our ship. The fog cleared just in the split second we needed to see and sink the five PT boats. The sixth one got away.

I'm convinced of this, that it was an answer to prayer that the fog cleared in the split second we needed to see and down the PT boats. My parents and grandparents as well as the church people were praying for my safety.

I'm alive. For fifty three years I've called that a miracle. And today, no one could convince me otherwise.

# CHAPTER 43

# Something Happened

## *Sam Hooker*

As kids, Leland Bryant and I lived a block apart. We were buddies. Leland's parents didn't attend church anywhere so Leland went with me. We went to Sunday school and then sat in church together. Being pretty bored, one thing we did to amuse ourselves was to count the times old Brother Chambers said "Dear Lord" in his prayers. One time it came up to thirty-eight. That was the record.

A big thing did get our attention though. A visiting minister preached on the wages of sin. This evangelist got into a big way when he described hellfire and how the poor sinners were cast into it.

These two little twelve-year-olds, got under conviction in a big way, too. When the altar call was given Leland and I, both trembling, walked up the aisle. We knelt at the altar bench. Pastor Woolman came down from the platform, gently counseled and prayed with us. Oh, we were under conviction, but bad and we repented, but good. When we stood up there were two little puddles of tears on the polished, white pine altar bench.

That particular Sunday there was a potluck dinner for the congregation right after church. We went down to the basement and stood in line. One of the women who missed church to help prepare for the meal, called to the lady in front of me, "Did anything happen in church this morning?"

Sister So-and-So answered in a casual voice, "No, not much."

Leland and I looked at each other with shocked faces. We thought something did happen in church that morning. We gave our hearts to Jesus! Wasn't that a big thing?

Well, fifty-one years went by. Leland and I lost track of each other. I moved to Portland, Oregon to go to Pacific Bible College and study for the ministry. Most of my years were spent on the West Coast. When our fortieth high school reunion came up, I decided to go. My wife chose not to. So I called the secretary who sent the invitation and asked if she had Leland Bryant's telephone number. She did.

I called Leland. He was pleased to hear from me and said, "You'll be going through my town of Peculiar, Missouri, on your way to Carthage. Stop and stay the night with me and my family."

I agreed.

"When you come through Peculiar, you'll see a telephone booth by a grocery store. It's the only one in our burg. Call me from it and wait there. I'll come get you."

I called and waited.

Soon a blue, Ford pickup truck rolled into the parking lot. I watched as a tall, lanky man in jeans unfolded himself and got out. We walked toward each other, reached out and embraced. Leland pushed me back to arms length, "Sam Hooker," he said with some emotion in his voice, "What have you done with your life?"

"I preached the gospel. Leland Bryant, what have you done with your life?"

"I preached the gospel."

With hesitancy Leland looked into my eyes, "I think something did happen in the church service that Sunday morning. Don't you?"

For several seconds we stood in silence as our minds went back to two young boys leaving small puddles of tears on the altar bench of a little, white church on Budlong and Orchard Streets in Carthage, Missouri.

# CHAPTER 44

# Confession of a
# Reformed Food Addict

## Lisa Hooker Belzac

Dinner time, July 17, 1987 was the landmark of my "bingeing days." My meal started with a complete package of Oreo Cookies. Following that came a bowl of chocolate Jell-o pudding made from a package that read "serves six." Even though my brain shouted, "Why? Why?" I kept shoveling down spoonful after spoonful of that sweet, creamy stuff until the bowl was clean. Then without being able to resist, I topped my meal off with a complete jumbo can of chilli con carne.

After that, I sat the 139 pounds of my 5' 3" frame down on the back porch of our upstairs apartment and hated myself for the sick, bloated fool I was. Soon I was on my way to where I could put my finger down my throat and bring up the ugly mess. As my foot hit the threshold of the bathroom door I stopped.

"Oh, God help me!" I shouted.

"You're stronger than that!" I heard a voice say, "You can beat this!"

I knew that voice came from God. I knew in my heart God would help me. My Gramma Mimi (Adele) taught me that I could trust him.

I scolded and shamed the gluttonous, immature girl inside me. Here I was, unable to have a loaf of bread sitting on the kitchen counter because I knew I'd eat the whole loaf at one time—when no one was looking, of course! I'd put bread into the refrigerator where I could get to it easily to eat between meals. Like a squirrel, I hid tasty morsels. Often I found them months later, dried out or moldy, as they lay hidden behind cans of chicken and tomato soup.

Now, ten years after my "great food binge," I can happily say, "With God's help I beat my enemy."

But not without strategy. I incorporated imagination and strict habit forming techniques. Here are some of the things God guided me to devise to save myself.

1. I always leave behind a small morsel of cake, pie, candy bar or whatever I'm eating.

When I realize I didn't eat the whole thing I know I don't have to start on another one.

2. I leave a basket of bread or rolls on the kitchen counter to show myself I don't have to eat whatever I see. (Now my husband can't understand why I consider this such a great accomplishment. He used to wonder why we were always out of bread.)

3. I stay super aware of how I eat, how much I put on my plate, how big a bite of food I put into my mouth.

4. I'm sensitive to the way other people eat. I observe them and evaluate their behavior.

This helps me to evaluate my own.

5. If I get the urge to binge, I check to see if there's something bothering me. Am I holding back from saying something I should to someone? I search my thoughts and feelings. If there is something I've left undone or someone I've offended, I seek out that person and talk with them, even if it's my mother on Mother's Day and at 1:00 a.m., as I did this year.

6. I meditate and pray a lot. I need God's help. I need strength beyond myself.

Breaking a devastating habit is a humungous job. Each person has to search out the ways that work for her- or himself. This is what worked for me. But it was God who first gave me the faith and courage to "work out my salvation with fear and trembling."—or rather with faith, persistence and discipline.

# CHAPTER 45

# The Monster

*Kimberly Davidson*

God turned my life-threatening food disorder into a pathway of service.

I was seventeen years old and obsessed with the thin-is-beautiful syndrome. Isn't that what TV, Hollywood and all the magazine adds tell us? If I'm thin I'll be beautiful, glamorous and happy. But the image of perfection created by our culture soon became a monster that controlled my life.

A friend told me how I could eat anything I wanted, lose however much weight I wanted and not gain an ounce back. It was so simple—just by self-induced vomiting. Within months bulimia became my choice of weight control. It was an effective tool. As the pressure of college increased and I ate to relieve it, my bulimia got worse. I added other popular tools to my stay-slim program: alcohol, cigarettes, diet pills, laxatives, diuretics. They all came to my aid.

After years of effort to create perfection, instead I created a monster.

It controlled my life. I saw myself: By day I was Ms. Jekyll, a college graduate, a smart business woman on the move. By night I was the Monster Hyde. I consumed pounds and pounds of food only to be followed by the high drama of a bathroom purge—head in toilet and other forms of elimination.

For sixteen years this monster called bulimia tortured me. With a many-stranded whip created of guilt, shame, fear, worthlessness, weakness and self-hatred, I scourged myself.

One day I met a godly man who invited me to church. There I faced the truth of who I was and how I dishonored the God-given-gift of a healthy body. This marvelous creation was designed to be a temple of the Living God. I made it a cesspool.

In bitter confession, humble repentance and faith-filled acceptance I gave my life to Jesus Christ. I claimed him as my Lord and Saviour. I asked forgiveness for self-centered pride and desire for popularity. I begged God for strength to win the battle over this self-created enemy.

Soon a strange thing came into view—I began to have a never-before desire to do crafts. My mind shifted from being thin and beautiful to being creative and productive. Without realizing it, food took a lesser place and the need to purge let up. A desire grew in me to honor God with all I had and was. I hungered to grow spiritually, which I did with the help of my friend and my church family. Something else grew—a desire within me to help others who were being held captive by this gluttonous and bingeing enemy. I became an inspirational speaker. I founded an eating disorder ministry called "Olive Branch Outreach." Now I'm advertised as "A Bulimia Survivor."

It's said of me, "Today Kim reaches out to hundreds of women to glorify the Lord Jesus Christ, and to make Him known by presenting Biblical solutions and teachings as part of her food-disorder healing ministry."

Now I am not only a survivor but I thrive on the joy of helping others escape this life-threatening monster. I praise God for his miracle in my life and that I can pass it on to others.

In case of you don't understand the gravity of bulimia, it kills. Many have been its victims.

# CHAPTER 46

# My Bright-Eyed Miracle

## *Darlene Goin*

My story starts with a dime.

My dime was lost and so was all hope of having an ice cream cone after the Sunday evening service at our Church of God camp ground. I paced back and forth on the porch of the little old shack that was the snack stand. Head down, I was intently looking for the dime I dropped. Perhaps it fell through one of the cracks between the weather beaten planks.

Soon I realized that someone else was scanning the porch floor with me. I looked up—straight into two beautiful, twinkling, blue eyes. There was an incredibly charming smile on the face with those eyes.

"I'm sure your dime is gone," he said after I told him what I was looking for, "and I don't have one to replace it. But here, I have a penny and I'll be back next Sunday to see if you still have it."

My heart beat fast at the sound of his mellow voice. And there was the hope of seeing him again in just one week.

Who was he? I didn't know.

I only knew I was taken in by his looks, his voice, his demeanor and now by his cleverness—what a line that was! And I swallowed it, "hook, line and sinker."

That was August, 1949, two weeks before my 14th birthday. I didn't know the age of the owner of those bright, blue eyes and I sure wasn't going to let him know how old—or young, I was. Later I learned he had just graduated from high school.

Sure enough, he came back to camp the next Sunday to check on the 1936 penny he gave me. I had it. From then on that penny was a subject of conversation that launched us into an exciting friendship.

Ardy Goin kept asking me how old I was. I kept evading the subject. I evaded it until I couldn't stall him off any longer. When I told him I was fourteen he almost lost his nerve. Silence pervaded the air.—too long for comfort.

When I feared I'd lost him entirely, he spoke up with resignation in his voice. "Well, I'll just have to get over it," he said. And he did.

We kept the mail flying for two years while he was in the army. By the time he came back I was at the fine, old age of seventeen and ready to be a married woman.

Ardith Lee Goin and Darlene Marian Flaming were married on June 28, 1953. For forty seven and a half years we were best friends, business partners and ardent lovers. We adored each other. All things we had in common: our religious beliefs, an electric wiring business and devotion to our five children. Together we made love and music. We made music for our church and on many special occasions Ardy performed solos with a heart-warming, mellow voice. I accompanied him. I also taught piano and organ lessons. We loved traveling and camping with our family and friends. I didn't think it would ever end. We'd grow old together in the warmth and devotion of each other's arms.

Things changed. Ardy became very ill. He could do little but sit painfully in a recliner and watch TV, in which he had little or no interest. Doctors were not able to turn the tide for us.

On a cold January afternoon in 2001, I stood with my grown children and their spouses around my darling's hospital bed. To cover our grief, we sang hymns, told family stories of years past, while we reluctantly ushered our beloved over the threshold and into that better place.

Oh, how jealous I was of all the departed family members and angels who welcomed my sweetheart in.

Ardith Lee had a twin brother named Arden Dee, nicknamed Dart for his speedy ways. I learned later that at about noon on that same fateful January day, when the doctor told me there was no hope for Ardy's recovery, Dart began feeling strange. Unable to concentrate on any work, he sat in front of the TV, feeling totally immobile.

His wife asked him if he were sick.

"No," he told her, "I don't feel sick—just "weird."

"I don't know what's wrong with me," he said.

Dart had no knowledge of the hospital drama we were engaged in. But suddenly at 4:30 that afternoon the strange feeling lifted. It was at 4:30 that very day that his twin brother, Ardy, passed into his new life.

******

The following Monday morning my cousin Marydith called. Two years earlier she lost her twenty-six-year-old son Joshua in an auto accident. At that time she told me of times and ways his spirit had seemed very near to her and she felt his "communication." On this morning she said she had a message for me.

She saw a vision. Joshua and Ardy were standing in heaven together. Joshua encouraged Marydith to be patient with his brother Brett in his drug and alcohol addictions.

"Everything is going to come out right in time," Joshua said.

Then Ardy told Marydith how wonderful it was up there. It seemed he was still in an attitude of amazement. Ardy sang a love song for me and expressed the hope that I would become open to his communication. Marydith sang the song to me over the phone. I'm a musician and have played hundreds of songs but this was beautiful beyond any song I ever heard.

Weeks went by, I missed my darling terribly.

One night I was lying in bed, unable to sleep. I was crying uncontrollably.

I said, "Oh, if you could just come love me one more time…"

I don't know if my eyes were open or closed, but I know that suddenly I saw him. His upper half appeared directly above the foot of my bed. He was in his prime again, with a full head of hair, wearing my favorite blue shirt. He did not have his beautiful smile, only a look of great compassion, tenderness and love. No words were spoken.

I cannot say how long it lasted, whether a minute or just seconds. I only know that peace washed over me. I ceased grieving and fell into a sound sleep.

This comforting scene is still imprinted on my mind.

On another occasion I was kneeling by my bed. Unable to pray, I only sobbed, "Help, help, help." It was the only thing I could pray in those bitter days.

As I sobbed on, I felt a continuing, rocking motion. Back and forth, back and forth it went in smooth, comforting rhythm.

When I stopped crying, I thought, Am I making myself rock? I don't think so.

When the feeling of being rocked back and forth diminished, I was sure I had not been physically rocked. Someone was holding me, rocking me and comforting me. My mind said, "My Lover came to comfort me."

******

On a Monday evening in March of that year, I was again lying in my bed in that twilight state of almost asleep. I heard a voice say, "Take care of our children." Again I heard it, but stronger, "Take care of our children." A third time, emphatically the words came, "Take care of our children." Sleepily I replied, "I'm trying, Honey." And I rolled over and went to sleep.

The time was around 10:00 P.M.

Unquestionably, I knew who was speaking. There is only one person with whom I have children.

Then another remarkable experience came in the form of a dream.

It was the same Monday night: Abruptly a figure appeared that looked like my youngest son when he was a teenager. The figure burst through my bedroom door, staggered toward me and collapsed on the floor. I awoke screaming, "Brian! Brian!"

My illuminated clock read 2:15 a.m. Was this dream a warning? Had something happened to my son? I decided to call his cell phone. I did, but got no answer.

Should I drive to where he lives? my mind asked. A sense came over me that I should just pray for him. I finally fell asleep praying.

When I awoke. A blitz of Brian's telephone number reverberated through my brain like the beat of a drum: boom—boom—boom! boom—boom—boom! boom—boom—boom .

What was I to do? It was 4:15 a.m.

Again I heard, "pray."

Then it was Tuesday morning: Brian's cheery voice answered the phone, "I'm just fine Mom. What's the matter?"

I explained.

Thursday evening: My daughter Laura called from her home 120 miles away. She told me on Monday evening she fought with her stepdaughter to keep her from running way. At 9:30 she had sent her to her room. Sometime between then and 10:00 P.M. the seventeen-year-old slipped out through her bedroom window. She went to a friend's house and then to a shelter for runaway kids. The shelter called. In those early morning hours two weary parents were trying to convince their daughter to come home. She refused.

Friday morning: I awoke with an urgent sense that I must call my daughter. Would my step-granddaughter, refusing to live at home, come live with me?

They asked, and she said, "Yes." She did.

—a strange story. Why was Brian and his phone number on my mind when he was not in trouble? Perhaps he was the one I had the greatest concern for and this was the person used to get my attention. This unusual dream definitely did get my attention and caused me to pray more earnestly than ever for our children.

\*\*\*\*\*\*

The sad and lonely months dragged on after my sweetheart's death. I sought some way to endure. Then the thought came into my mind, All the experiences you've had should tell you I am still aware and caring for you. You needed to give thanks to God and me for that.

I felt I needed to focus on the wonderful forty-seven-and-a-half years that we had together in a beautiful love song. I needed to develop a constant attitude of gratitude for my family of five children with spouses and grandchildren, for my pleasant home, for twenty seven piano students that gave me great joy and the fact that I had a way to make a living, also for the business he left for my son and me to cooperate in. I was blessed with so much.

I was being told I needed to focus with gratitude on what I did have and stop pitying myself for what I didn't have.

Also, I was told to say, "Thank you, God, that Ardy is pain free and stress free. He is in a wonderful environment without any more health worries."

This I did. And soon it became natural for me to talk to Ardy as though he were still with me.

One day I was walking about in the kitchen doing my work. I said, "Well, what are you doing now, Honey? Are you flying around, visiting all the places we dreamed of traveling to? Seeing the world? How nice to have your own wings, and not have to catch a plane, or..."

Shocked! I heard, out of somewhere, beyond myself, one word, "Growing."

"Growing?!" I said. "Do they make you go to classes up there?"

Then I was told that we, here, know so little about there.

Surprises galore are in store for us, I was told.

I can't wait!

# CHAPTER 47

# I'm Not in the Morgue!

## *A. H.*

I got up this morning because I'm not in the morgue.

I still tremble at the thought of where I could be at this very moment were it not for the grace of God that saved me from a fateful auto-accident.

Because of Sam's bad hearing, I went to the dentist with him. His appointment was at 11:15 a. m. There was Margaret LaFont's funeral to attend at 1:00 P.M.

"Dr. King is squeezing me in so I'm sure he'll just check my tooth today and have me come in to do the rest later," Sam said. "I'm not going with you to the funeral. I'd like to. But I can't hear and my mouth hurts, bad."

Well, the dentist decided to start a root canal. That put us out of his office at 12:05. I was in my grubbies. I had to go home and change. It was a 25 minute drive home and a 25 minute drive back to the church, if we hurried. I rushed to change my clothes in five minutes and then rushed on my way to the church. I knew I'd be late, but didn't want to be terribly late to the funeral.

So here I was, rushing down highway I 205 in the far-left lane at 65 miles per hour. The car ahead of me blocked my view. I did not see the large box in the middle of my lane until the other car swerved to the left, around it. I had a split second for two thoughts; swerve left toward the shoulder and ram the other car or swerve right into the next lane. I swerved right with hope.

Only by God's grace, was there no car in the lane beside me and none coming up close behind. It was a busy highway. A few yards ahead and a few yards back the cars were moving close together and with speed. Only for those few seconds was the next lane free of traffic for my use.

How I thank God for saving me—life and limb.

Still—another thought comes to mind, a comforting thought. I could be up playing with the angels now. This is no small comfort when we realize how quickly we can be snatched from this earth. But since I still have books to write and family to love and care for, I thank the good Lord that I'm not up there "playing a harp."

And, I'm not in a morgue.

# CHAPTER 48

# No Formula for Miracles

## *Nola Olson*

Lying on the gurney in the emergency room in excruciating pain, I was curled up in a ball. The doctor and my husband, Alan, were in the hall discussing the cause of my severe pain. The doctor thought I was passing a large kidney stone through the small tube, to the bladder. The nurse gave me a shot to dull the pain.

I was six to eight weeks pregnant. My regular gynecologist turned me over to another GYN who handled problematic and high risk pregnancies.

At eight months, I was again hospitalized with a kidney stone too large to pass. It was embedded and would not move.

Pain from the stone, infection and swelling never went away. The stones I had were said to be of non-specific origin. Therefore, there was no determined treatment to dissolve them. I was continually on medication for pain. How would this affect the baby I was carrying? That was my deep and constant concern. But, thanks be to God, to my great relief Jonathan was born a very healthy baby weighing seven pounds and eleven ounces.

When he was just five days old I was rushed to hospital again. Each time I went to the hospital my one-year-old son and my five-year-old daughter were "farmed out" to stay with friends. Now my sister, Donna took infant Jonathan. Donna had two children of her own and an infant added much to her load. I was oh, so grateful for her generosity but worried over my having put this added burden onto her. This and fretting to be away from my children, added to my already troubled mind over the excruciating pain. I'm sure it didn't help my body chemistry.

Family and friends were ever so kind. First was Donna's big heart to care for my children. And there was my friend, Peggy. She allowed me to breast feed baby Jonathan. In the hospital I drew the milk from my breasts, the staff kept it fresh by freezing it and Peggy did milk runs. Every day she came to the hospital, picked up the milk and took it to Donna's house.

In addition to my supportive family, my whole church was praying for me.

I don't know why God doesn't answer prayer more quickly, I thought. He must have his own reasons. Is he growing us up this way? I know he can heal.

Sometimes I wondered if he heard me. Oh, how often I've prayed, "Lord, I believe. Help my unbelief." At this particular time I had a whole lot more unbelief than belief. In fact, I quit praying for myself. While I was in the hospital with "The Big Stone" Donna and her husband Bob came to see me. They were convinced of a "Name it and Claim it" method of praying. The Scripture does say, "Ask in my name and it shall be given unto you." But to me, "Name it and Claim it" seemed to be a fad among the Pentecostal churches.

I have many Pentecostal and charismatic friends. I treasure them all and do not argue with their beliefs. However, that type of praying doesn't seem to fit my nature. I respect their following the leadings they feel are right for them.

But I have seen incidents where the "Name it and Claim it" formula did not produce a healing. My mother was a prime example of this.

Donna, Ray and their children agreed to pray that way. They asked God to give Mama a new heart. She had suffered with heart ailment for many years. But Mama died of a heart attack. So, at that time, although Donna wanted me to pray her way, I just couldn't feel that method was right for me, so I prayed, "Thy will be done, Lord." Donna felt that wasn't showing much faith.

In my terrible pain, when Donna and Ray came to the hospital to pray for me, I didn't object to their method. I had so little faith for myself, I appreciated any prayers regardless of the manner in which they were given.

My brother-in-law laid his hand on my abdomen and prayed a "Name it and Claim it" prayer. "Stone be crushed in the name of Jesus!" he said.

I didn't feel any change. I kept taking the medication.

When I was out of the hospital, Alan and I attended a Bible study. We were assigned to read the entire book of Matthew. In it I kept reading where Jesus said to people, "As your faith so be it unto you." He anointed and prayed for them. Then he told each of them to do a different thing. Lepers he told to go wash in the pool of Bethesda. One man he told to go show himself to the priest and take an offering. It seemed he never did his healings the same way. One time he even anointed a blind person's eyes with clay he made with spittle. I couldn't see a formula in Jesus' manner of healing.

Three things I did observe; Jesus usually touched them, but not always. He prayed to the Father, and he told them to do something which they obeyed. It seemed faith, prayer and obedience were three constants. I felt I didn't have the faith. But I was beginning to feel more and more that I should go to the altar of the church, be anointed and prayed for. This would be my act of obedience.

One day my family was at our house. We were sitting at the table having dinner together. I told them I was scheduled for surgery and that I'd need places for the children to stay while I was in the hospital. My five-year-old daughter burst into tears and shouted, "I don't want to go stay anywhere. I just want to stay home." It broke my heart.

That night I told Alan, "I want to go to the altar of the church, be anointed and prayed for. I need to be obedient to what I know."

"Next Sunday, Honey, we'll go forward to the altar," Alan said.

In the meantime, one morning my friend, Peggy, called.

She was excited. "Nola," she said, "last night I went to a meeting to hear a minister who has the gift of healing. He said for any one who wanted to come down and be prayed for or for another person who needed to be healed, we could do so. I went down to the front of the church and stood in your stead. When the minister touched me I fell down. The Spirit of God was so strong I couldn't move. Did you feel anything Friday night?" Peggy asked.

"No, I didn't feel anything." I answered honestly even though I knew she'd be disappointed. Which I sensed she was.

At church the next Sunday the visiting minister spoke of Jesus' healing. He invited people to come to the front and be prayed for. He said, "If you don't have the faith, that's all right, I do. Come and I'll pray for you."

Ah, I thought, I don't need to have faith, he'll have faith for me. I took hope.

Alan and I walked down to the altar and knelt. One of our ministers came to me. He anointed my forehead with oil, laid his hand on my head and said a prayer.

Did I feel any thing? No.

Nothing happened. I had to continue my medication.

But something did happen. I was amazed at the fact that each day I became more and more sure that I was healed. Each day I could feel myself growing in faith. Alan's faith grew in the same way.

Two weeks later I was in the hospital again. This time to have X-rays in preparation for the scheduled surgery to remove that big, embedded kidney stone. The surgeon wanted to be sure it was exactly where it was before so he would find it when he did the surgery. The stone could have moved and made the surgery more complicated. X-rays would pinpoint the location.

I lay under the X-rays machine and "knew." I was sure they wouldn't find the stone. I knew the technician would come in and say. "Mrs. Olson, I'm sorry we're going to have to take other X-rays. We can't find the kidney stone."

I was so sure she'd say that, that when she came back and said, "Okay, you can go now." I said "What?!"

She said, "Oh, you want to know the results? I'll go ask the doctor who's reading the X-rays."

I went out and joined Alan in the waiting room. When the technician came out she had a smile on her face and said, "Everything is fine."

"But what about the kidney stone I'm supposed to have surgery for in a week?" I asked.

"Kidney stone? Is that what we're supposed to find?" she queried. "I'll have to go back and talk to the doctor again."

When she came back she said, "I talked to the doctor and he said he has moved on to the other X-rays and can't go back and look at yours, but the ureter is wide open and everything is normal."

Alan and I laughed and hugged. We knew the Lord had healed me. We went home, got someone to stay with the children and went out to celebrate. We went to dinner and then to a little gift shop. We wanted to find an "Ebeneezer." That's a tangible something to commemorate an Epiphany, a manifestation of God's Presence. In this little craft shop we found the very right thing, a plaque with two people walking together on the beach by the ocean. One person in a white robe is obviously Jesus. But then there are only one set of footprints. Did Jesus leave ? At the side, printed over the water, are the words of the poem, "Footprints In The Sand."

How fitting it was! Jesus carried me when I didn't have strength or faith to carry myself. On the back of the plaque I penned these words,

PRAISE THE LORD!
To commemorate the Lord Healing
me of my kidney stone
October 10, 1985
Nova Olson

Three days later the doctor's secretary called to tell me the surgery was canceled. She said, "You must have passed the stone."

"No," I said, "I didn't pass it. It was embedded and wouldn't move and it was too big to pass."

"It must have fallen apart and you passed the gravel."

"Ma'am, I have passed kidney stones in this past year and I know what it feels like to pass kidney stones. Now I have been totally free from pain."

Poor soul, she didn't know what to do with me. She got frustrated and in an upset tone of voice she said, "Well, I don't understand!"

"I know you don't understand," I said, "but my husband and I do. We're Christians. And we know that the Lord reached out his hand and touched me."

She mumbled something and hung up. Obviously she was uncomfortable with truth that she didn't know about.

My mind has mused over it all. I've asked myself, Now when did I get healed? Was it when Bob said, 'Stone be crushed, in Jesus' name'?

Was it when Peggy stood in for me and was touched by the power of the Spirit to where all her own energy was gone out of her body and she fell down and couldn't move? Was that the time of my healing?

Was it when I knelt at the altar in obedience and the minister anointed and prayed for me? Was it then?

I don't know. And I'm glad I don't know. This way I won't give praise and glory to a method or a formula. All my praise goes to the God who healed me.

Now, in all the twenty years since then, I have not had one kidney stone.

That a large, embedded kidney stone vanishing completely, is a miracle of healing and a great gift. But that our weak, quavering faith is enlarged and solidified for eternity is a far greater gift and a miracle beyond expression.

And, oh yes! We learned much in our year of confusion, trial and suffering. We learned to keep hope and faith alive and for sure, obedience is of great value.

# CHAPTER 49

# "Buying a Camel?"

## *A. H.*

"Buying a camel? So you're taking up smoking, huh? Gonna buy a pack of cigarettes?" That's the general remark a man would say when I broached the subject of my new missionary adventure. At least it got their attention when I told them I was buying a camel.

"No," I'd say, "I'm buying a real live camel."

"And where will you keep your camel? In the garage?"—usually their next question.

I hit up family, friends and even total strangers at the mall where my husband Sam and I walked each morning. You see I got this crazy idea that I could buy a camel with other peoples' money. I'd have to raise five-hundred-dollars, the price of a camel, by sharing my story and asking for just one single dollar from each "customer." It would take patience and some endurance, but I could do it. I really believed that. I must admit I can be rather persistent and my husband says, "pushy."

Okay, I admit I can be pushy if I really believed in the cause.

And what was my cause? A camel for a needy Masaai tribe in Tanzania.

You see, as far back as I can remember I've had a heart for Africa. As a child my most exciting church services were when missionaries spoke. Something stirred in me when I was a teenager. Maybe God wanted me to go to Africa and teach the children about Jesus. That was a persistent thought. It influenced me to go on to college. I attended Pacific Bible College (now Warner Pacific College in Portland, Oregon). There I met and married Sam Hooker, a young ministerial student, and became a pastor's wife. Sam had no drawing to Africa. But I never lost my heart for this country with so many needy people.

Years later, Sam and I travelled to Kima, Africa. When we came home to our Woodstock Church of God in Portland, Oregon, we raised $10,000 and recruited five of our members to join a group who went to Kenya to build a church.

I've given our kids goats for Christmas. Their gift-money was sent to buy goats in my children's names. Goat-Randy's picture, is still on my refrigerator door. At one time Sam's and my Christmas presents to each other was money sent to Peru to buy two goats. "Would you name them Sam and Adele and let them have baby goats to give to needy families?" Now after these twenty years I wonder how many children have had milk because "Sam and Adele" were sent to Peru.

Lately a video was shown at my church, Mt. Scott Church of God, picturing the Masaai tribe and their need for camels. I'd already visited with some of these tall, slender warriors and I liked them.

"I want to buy a camel for the Masaai tribe." I told Sam.

"You're already supporting Children of Promise and Scholarships for KIST (Kima Institute of Theological Studies) Isn't that's enough?" he said.

"I just want to buy a camel. I think that would be fun."

"I think we're doing plenty."

I pondered it.

Ah! Then it hit me. I could hear myself talk to myself.

"Adele, you're 83 years old. If you don't have 500 friends and acquaintances by now, you haven't lived well. If each one gave just a dollar you'd have five hundred dollars to buy your camel."

That stirred a peck of excitement in me.

"Ho, ho, ho!" I said to me, "I'm gonna buy a camel!"

So I started telling everyone I could that I was buying a camel.

"You're what?!" they expostulated. (That means "demanded earnestly.") "You're going to do what?!"

And I'd relate my animated tale.

"The Masaai tribe in Africa are tall, slender nomads who live on milk and blood. They bleed the cow a bit and mix the blood with milk. That is their staple food. Cows go dry during gestation but camels, also their beasts of burden, give milk the year round. Too, a camel is the only known animal whose milk contains vitamin C. The Masaai children are deficient in vitamin C. For just one dollar you can invest in a Camel. Isn't that exciting?! In fact, you can buy three hairs from a camel's tail for two dollars."

Rarely did anyone say, "I don't have a dollar on me." Several people gave me bigger bills, 5, 10, 20. My precious and warm hearted niece, Linda Smith, brought a hundred dollar bill to my house. "Here, this is for your camel," she said. Several other times she handed me a 20. She and her daughter set a "camel-fund-jar" on their kitchen counter where they put their change. It amounted to $36. 28. By this time she was calling it "our camel."

When I asked my wonderful neighbor, Mark Brackett, for a dollar, he said, "Oh no! If I have a chance to invest in a camel, it's gonna be more than a dollar." He handed me a fifty and said, "How much of the fella will that buy? And I don't want any of the tail end!"

"How about the hump?" I said.

In a small group when I was telling my camel story and nobody budged, dear Jan Barber took pity on me. She said, "Adele, how much more do you need?" I said, "I think forty dollars will do it." She reached for her purse. I thought, "Oh, I'll bet she gives me a ten.?" But no. It was her check book that came out and I was forty dollars ahead. When I got home and counted, I was just one dollar short of buying my camel. I collected that from Amelia, my one-year-old great-grand-baby who lives next door.

For seven years Sam and I have walked the Clackamas Town Center

Mall. We've become acquainted with many of the mall-walkers. One of the men, Doug, got a kick out of hollering to me when I was talking to someone else, "Hey Adele, did you get a dollar from him for your camel?"

That gave me the opportunity to make my pitch.

You may ask, "Where's the miracle in this story?"

I see several of them.

1. Why should an 83 year old woman want to take on the job of asking 500 people for a dollar?

2. Why worry about a stranger in a foreign country and his need for a beast of burden?

3. Why should one be concerned about African children having milk with vitamin C in it when millions of children around the world have no milk?

4. Why care at all?

My answer is this. A miracle is a happening that would not exist without a superior power being involved. That God gave me the thought in the first place and then the faith that I could endure long enough to talk to five hundred people if need be, asking them each for a dollar, that astounds me when I think of it.

Where did I get the guts or grit to approach total strangers, friends and family and ask for money! I can hardly believe that of myself. I even have to pat myself and God on the back for the persistence I had to keep at the project for well over a year and see it to the finish.

I surprise myself.

And you can believe the folks at our church missionary board were surprised when they got a packet of 500 one dollar bills marked, "For a camel in Tanzania."

That we are workers together with God can be a lot of fun. My camel buying was.

# CHAPTER 50

# Jason's Story

## *Jason Lutz*

"Jason Lutz," I said on the phone, "this is Mimi. (my gramma name) I have to have your story. Bob told you I'm writing a book of miracles. I've got nearly fifty, yours tops them all. When can I get it?"

"I'm free Monday morning."

"OK. I'll have breakfast ready at ten. Be here."

That's how our relationship started. Our mutual friend Bob Lynn told me about Jason and told Jason about me. It was an immediate hit. God was in it.

Monday, at ten, Jason and I had Jimmie Dean sausages, fried potatoes, eggs (Jason ate three), toast, strawberry jam (home made) and coffee. With mouths full, we did small talk. As soon as our plates were empty, I scooted the dishes away, took out the pad I had handy with two soft-lead pencils and an electric pencil sharpener. "I don't do shorthand but I do fast scribble," I said to Jason.

I asked him a question. He started talking, and away we went!

\*\*\*\*\*

So you were in prison—7 1/2 years. Tell me about it.

I spent eight years in lock up, seven and a half in prisons—five different ones. I started out, headed that way from a kid. I smoked at the age of nine, by eleven I was drinking and using marijuana. My brother and I were always pounding on each other.

>Hey, hold it. Where were your parents all this time that you got away with that?

I didn't have a dad. Mom loved us and was a good mother, but she worked two 'n three jobs to support the five of us. My grandmother took care of us kids. She disciplined us. But it didn't do much good. I look back and try to analyze my situation. I think life was boring to me. I created trouble to make it interesting. At least it seems that way now.

By nineteen I was high most of the time using "meth". That's amphetamine. You know it as speed and crack. At twenty one I managed a Taco Bell with thirteen Mexicans under me. That's when I got involved with this guy named Caesar. He was a drug dealer at the party where I went to buy stuff.

>What kind of party?

A party is a house or an apartment where everyone's using drugs. You go to make a deal. You know who to buy from. You say something like this, "I'm looking for some bud or green, that's marijuana. If it's meth you want you say, "I'm looking for tweak" ( or dope) Meth users are called tweakers. When enough of it gets in you, you're baked out of your brain.

I didn't take to heroin—slows you down. I'm a high energy guy. I went for stuff that speeded me up.

Caesar and I'd go into another room, outside or in the car, make the exchange—cash for dope, and split. If the party-goings-on interested me, I'd hang out or join the thing I wanted to do. There's usually TV, some guitar playing, drawing, doing crafts or just tweaking. Tweaking is fiddling with anything in your hands or just sitting stoned out of your mind, fiddling with your own fingers. Sex was going on in another room or two. At a party, it doesn't matter what you're doing. Nobody cares about anyone else. I've seen a body stretched out with a blanket over it. It could be sleeping or dead. Life has little value to druggers.

After buying from Caesar for a while, we became friends—I say that lightly. In the drug culture you don't have friends. You can't really trust anyone. We started hanging out together every day. At first I had an apartment. Then I rented a house and three of us guys and one girl. lived together. We all used drugs. Caesar dealt. I covered half of his rent for my drugs. He gave me all the meth I needed.

I worked full time at Taco Bell—often sixty hours a week. I didn't care. Mostly I was high so time went quick. I couldn't sleep anyway. On meth your mind's jumping. Sometimes I'd go a week or two without sleep.

Caesar and I hung out together for about a year. He introduced me to cocaine. On cocaine my life really started to go crazy. I got paranoid. Started carrying a pistol.

>Where?

On my waist band or in my tote bag.

What did I have in my tote bag? Stuff. All kinds of junk: papers, receipts, books, wrenches, screw drivers, pipes, snorter tools, photos, day planner—just a bunch of junk. My possessions! Sometimes I carried my pistol in my tote bag.

On cocaine, I was of a mindset that if someone even looked at me wrong I'd punch them out or just shoot them. I shot at a few people. Guess God was looking out for me, 'cause I never hit anyone—with the gun that is. I hit plenty guys with my fists. I was quick with my anger and fists. I liked to take on bullies. I've always had a soft spot for underdogs. If I saw a bully messing with a weaker person, I'd relish the fun of beating him up or just knocking him out.

My Taco Bell pay wasn't enough for Caesar and me. We started hitting people up at ATMs. That way we could go from one location to another and throw the cops off. We wore ski masks so people couldn't identify us. We did some house robberies, took stereos, computers, jewelry. Didn't usually find much cash.

Did we take credit cards? Nope. Too much trouble. Too much work. We were looking for quick cash. Cops never got me for any of that stuff. I was caught because I robbed my own restaurant, my Taco Bell.

Caesar was getting cocaine from the Mexican Mafia. I didn't know it. He ran up a $3,000 bill and was hiding out. When they couldn't find him they came after me. I didn't know one of my workers was a Mafia guy. Of the thirteen Mexicans that worked for me only two spoke English. One worked out front and the other spelled me off at the drive-in. I spoke enough Spanish to get by.

Jimmie (name changed) from Mafia, came to me at work. He said, "I want the money."

I said, "I don't have it."

He showed me a piece of paper with my mother's and grandmother's addresses on it.

"I'll go see them."

I knew what he meant.

"I'll have the money in two days."

"I want it tomorrow."

"I need a day to plan. I'll have it for you the day after tomorrow."

"Day after tomorrow. I'll be here."

He turned and walked away.

I went home and there was Caesar. I was mad at him but he was crying. Like I told you, I always had a soft spot for someone hurting. It was God's call on my life, but I didn't know it. So Caesar and I planned the robbery together.

He'd come to the Taco Bell with ski mask and gun and hold me up. Monday nights were slow. I sent all the employees home but one. Before time for Caesar, I sent him to the back to wash dishes. At midnight, as planned, Caesar came in by the side door. My employee came out front and Caesar held us both up. He took the employee's wallet, although I asked him not to. I put all the money from the safe and till into money bags. Caesar took it and left.

I called the police. They came. Told them we'd been robbed and gave a fake description of Caesar. Since my employee didn't speak English he didn't know it was fake. They questioned the employee but he couldn't understand them. The police left.

I went home. Caesar and I split the money and gave some to the driver of the car. He was a seventeen-year-old-runaway living with us. I met him at a party. He needed a place to stay. I got him a job at another Taco Bell and he was selling drugs for me on the side. We gave Caesar more than we took so he could pay the $3,000 debt. But he didn't pay it. He took the $3,000 and bought more dope from somebody else.

A cop came back to the Taco Bell the next day and brought an interpreter. They talked to my employee. He described the robber different from me. That got suspicions up. A detective was put on my trail. He followed me every where, watched where I spent money—in hotels, bars, known drug houses. He got to know who I hung out with: Caesar, his fiance, my fiance and Dustin, the boy.

Dustin's parents had reported their runaway son. The police spotted his license plate and pulled him over on the highway. They took him to the juvenile detention center and took his car to his parents. Later, his parents opened the trunk and found the deposit bags, ski mask and gloves. They took these to the Taco Bell where Dustin worked. The Taco Bell manager gave them to the police who questioned Dustin. He wouldn't tell them anything. In the car they found his pager. On the pager was Caesar's fiances number. She was already in trouble by selling drugs to an undercover cop. They went to see her, told her she was in trouble. If she didn't tell them everything, they'd put her in prison. She told.

The police came to my fiances house and asked me to come in for questioning. They showed me pictures of money bags, ski mask, gloves and asked me what I knew about them. Said I didn't know anything about them. They asked if I knew Caesar. Said I didn't.

"The detective saw you together."

I asked for a court appointed lawyer. She came and asked me to tell her my story. I told her the truth because I knew she couldn't use it against me. She could only advise me.

"They have all the evidence on you," she said. "It calls for measure eleven, the mandatory minimum prison sentence of 90 months. There's no way around it. Unless you want to take the deal."

The police offered me a deal—reduced sentence of three years if I testified against my crime partners.

"No way!" I said. "I'm not rattin' on anybody."

They handcuffed me and walked me to a cell.

I went on trial with three charges: theft, robbery and unlawful use of fire arms. A jury found me guilty. I was put back in my jail cell.

The night before I was to go to prison I decided to commit suicide. I tied one end of my sheet to the upper part of the cell bars. The other end I tied around my neck. I was up on the sink ready to jump when someone pulled on my pant leg. I looked down and there was a little, old, curly, gray-haired man reaching through the bars.

"You don't have to do that," he said. "Let me tell you about Jesus."

I was so mad at him for keeping me from killing myself that I cussed him out good—or bad. I jumped onto my bunk and covered my head with the blanket. When I uncovered my head he was gone.

About an hour later the guard came by. I asked to see the chaplain.

"There's no chaplain here tonight." the guard said.

"Yes. He's here. I was just talking to him."

"You're wrong. He's not here. It's his day off."

"Well, I want to talk to that little, old, gray-haired man that I was talking to an hour ago. He wears small, round-framed glasses and he's got short, curly, gray hair and bright, bright, blue eyes. I know he's here because I just talked to him."

"No one's here that fits that description. We had trouble up stairs and the jail's on lock down. No one's been in or out. We're all locked up."

I knew I talked to the man 'cause I'll never forget his eyes. They were a unique blue—real, real bright, yet soft, an ocean blue. Although I was mad as hell and cursed him out, he was peaceful. I can't forget the way he looked at me.

Then I went to bed. Strangely I fell right to sleep and slept peacefully until morning when the jail staff came to get me for transport.

In a van with steel cage grating they took me to OSCI, "Oregon State Correctional Institute" in Salem. In the three months I was there I got into fifteen fights. Inmates try to provoke each other. I never took down-talk off anybody. Not even when I was a kid. Wouldn't let anybody talk bad about me or my family.

When I was about five, a neighbor kid threw a rock at me. It hit me and I bled. I ran over, knocked him down and beat on him until his mother screamed at me to stop. She called the police. Police came to our house, talked to my mom. I stayed in my room. She gave me a spanking and I laughed. My mother never knew what to do with me.

With that fight I realized it felt better to beat on other kids than on my brother. He and I would fight a lot. Now I found plenty of others to beat up on. I had an issue with bullies. I'd take them on three or four times my size. I never picked on weaker kids. No, never. Wasn't my style.

In prison, I picked on bullies, too. There, murderers are held in high esteem. The ones in for murder, robbery, theft, beat up on those in for rape or child abuse. I couldn't see it. We all hurt people, just in different ways. The bullies picked on the others, strong-armed them, took away anything they wanted: radios, tooth paste, canteen stuff, things their family sent. I was always ready for a fight and I found plenty causes.

In Salem they took the trouble makers, five hundred of us, and sent us to CCA, "Corrections Corporations of America," a privately owned prison in Florence, Arizona. There's a number of them throughout the country. Seven thousand of us wore different colors according to the states we came from.

Here I got a job in the kitchen as a grunt cook.

>A grunt cook?

A fetch cook. He does all the menial tasks like opening cans, getting tools for the cook, carrying out the garbage, stuff like that. The cooks taunt a grunt cook. They made fun of me. It gave me lots of reason to fight. I knew I was a better cook than any of them. My uncle's a gourmet cook. He cooks at a golf club in Oregon. I hung out with him and learned to cook. I don't measure things—go by feel, taste 'n smell.

Too, I was in witchcraft for five years, carried a heavy yoke on my back, always mad.

>In witchcraft, what does that mean?

I practiced sorcery, put spells on people with the supernatural power of evil spirits. I used incantations I learned from spell books.

Always had a heavy weight on my back, my shoulders, mad all the time, never at peace. Didn't know what peace was, not even the term.

Then I met Russell Thomas.

He was a specialty cook—did the low-salt, vegetarian, diabetes diets. He asked me if I wanted to be his assistant; he'd split his duties with me.

195

No more constant belittling as a grunt cook. I'd be a specialty cook, his equal, their equal.

I did the diet trays: vegetarian, low salt, no pork, no beef, liquid diet. Each tray had a different color on the meal cart.

For six months I worked with Russell and immediately disliked him. He was an excellent cook but I hated the way he acted. He smiled all the time. He was happy. He even laughed. Man, that made me mad! I came to work all fired up. I thought, You're in prison just like me. What the hell you happy about?

One day I asked him what he was happy about. He said it was because of Jesus and he put his hand on my shoulder. That was a big mistake. I didn't let anybody touch me. I grabbed his arm and pushed him against the wall and told him I never, never wanted him to talk to me about Jesus. I had a butcher knife in my hand. I wanted to shove it into his stomach. But something kept me from it.

Then he had the gall to ask me if I wanted to know about God.

He put his hand on my forearm and soft-spokenly said, "Just let me tell you about God."

Oh, was I mad! He wasn't even afraid! I wanted to punch him. Couldn't. Something stopped me.

I hated Christians. Just hated Christians. I had an uncle that I loved and respected. I wanted his approval. He was a Christian, even a pastor. He wouldn't have anything to do with us. Wouldn't let his family have anything to do with our family. That hurt me so bad. From then on I hated all Christians.

My normal reaction to Russell was to nail him! He wouldn't know what hit him. But I couldn't. I was stopped cold.

Now I know it was angelic presence. Didn't know it then.

Next morning walking to work I thought, If he smiles one more time I'll knock his teeth out. I got there and he just kinda smiled and said, "Ya know Bro, I'll just keep prayin' for ya."

I wanted to stick the knife into his belly, but somehow I couldn't. Russell didn't even flinch.

"Don't be prayin' fer me!" I barked at him, "keep your prayers to yerself. Prayin' don't do any good 'cause there ain't no God. It couldn't help anybody, 'specially me."

Very kindly Russell said, "Common, we've got work to finish."

I thought, Why isn't he mad? I just threatened to put a knife into him. And why wasn't he scared? He knows my reputation—that I liked to take on big guys. And Russell was a really big guy—just the kind I liked to put down.

The look in his eyes, I didn't understand it. It was like something I didn't know anything about. It penetrated all through me. Now I know it was pure love. I didn't know it then. I'd never seen it before.

We ended our shift without talking and I went home to my cell. Then thought I'd go down and watch some TV. These hardened criminals usually watch immoral shows, girly 'n stuff like that. But for some reason, every channel they switched to had something about God. Finally they settled on "Touched By An Angel." That made me madder'n ever! I went home and went to bed.

I put my head phones on and listened to the radio. Fell asleep that way. About midnight a voice woke me up. It called my name, "Jason."

I looked around. No cell mates were up. I pulled the pillow tight over my head and tried to go back to sleep. The voice again—it said, "Jason wake up. Jason, I'm talking to you."

It was my voice, but not my words. I wouldn't call my own name and tell myself I was talking to myself. Weird!

Then the voice said, "I'm here to git you."

I'm thinking, Am I going crazy? I must be going mad 'cause I'm hearing voices now.

I said, "Shut up! I don't want to listen to you."

The voice was quiet.

That sparked my curiosity. I wondered if I really heard someone or if I was going nuts. If I really heard someone, who was it?

I said, "Who are you anyway?"

He said, "I'm Jesus, your Lord."

Russell's picture popped into my mind. And Oh, I was fightin' mad!

I told God, "I'm not talking to you any more. I know all about you already."

God said, "Jason, we're done with this life."

"What do you mean, done with this life? I'm only twenty three years old, I'm young and healthy."

I was up to 140 pounds from 125 when I went into prison. At five-foot-nine, 125 pounds was pretty scrawny. But I was tough, all muscle. (Now I'm 197.)

Lord said, "Doesn't matter what you say or think. Nothing will change the outcome of tonight."

"What do you mean?" I yelled it loud in the silence of my own mind.

That's when the Lord started barking his commands at me. His voice boomed in my head like a loud speaker. "No more asking questions. Now it's time for you to listen. Get off your bunk and pray to me."

I argued with God.

"No, I don't have to do what you tell me to."

I started to feel sharp pains in the left side of my chest.

"You need to get down now and accept me as Lord."

"No way! I'm not gonna do it."

The left side of my body went numb. Couldn't feel it. Couldn't move my left leg.

I'm having a heart attack! I thought.

"If you don't get down and pray to me you won't wake up in the morning."

My heart was beating so hard I thought it was gonna bust right out of my chest. Head hurt, throbbed hard with sweating 'n fever. I was scared, really scared. Was I gonna die? First time in my life I felt fear. Never was 'fraid of anything. When my mother spanked me I'd laugh at her. Never would cry. Now I knew I was having a heart attack, gonna die!

"I can't get down. The guys'll make fun of me."

"I promise you they won't even wake up."

For some reason I trusted the voice. First time I trusted anybody. Even as a little kid, long as I could remember, everyone let me down. My mom—wanted her love but got spankings. She was a good mother, loved us kids and wanted the best for us. Looking back I realize I did mean things to get spanked. Guess I was an attention and excitement freak. Life was too dull. I'd pay the price to get things goin'. Had no dad. Felt no one cared much. Maybe my grandma, a little. Why did I know I could trust the one whose voice I heard? Don't know, but I did.

I made a decision. Decided I'd do it.

Then my heart stopped beating hard. Could move my leg. Chest pain gone. I jumped out of my bunk, knelt down on the cold, hard concrete and immediately started to cry—hadn't cried in years.

"I don't know how to pray to you." I said it softly.

That's when I knew it was God 'cause I never spoke soft to anybody.

"I know your heart." God spoke back—ever so softly.

I was cryin' bad. There was a heavy weight on my shoulders. It was pushing me down lower and lower. All of the years of pain and heartache: emotional abuse, drug abuse, heavy burden of witch craft. I cast spells on people I hated. Somehow I'd get an item of theirs—lock of hair, saliva, drop of blood. Put it in cigarette papers and do an incantation over it—repeated words I learned from spell books. Then I'd burn it, blow over it and pour water on it—gods of fire, wind and water—all just demons, but I didn't know it then.

How often did I do that? Maybe three or four times a month to people who treated me bad: drug dealers who cheated me, anyone who put me down, embarrassed me in front of others. All that stuff together—that was the weight, a crippling weight, heavy on my shoulders.

First I was on my knees. The weight kept pushing me down farther and farther until I was on my chest, then flat out on my belly and face on the hard, cold concrete. Weight so heavy I couldn't hold my body up. It was crushing the life out of me. I was crying and snotting.

Then I heard the kind, gentle voice quietly say, "My burden is light."

"If you could just take this weight away for a minute."

"If you trust in me, you don't have to bear it—unless you choose to."

"Oh! What do I have to do?"

"Just accept me as Lord and Saviour."

I knew about Jesus dying on the cross from when I went to church with my grandmother—knew, but didn't accept.

Just so quick I believed. "I accept you Jesus and believe that you died on the cross for me."

That quick. And the burden was gone. I could breathe. For the first time in my life I could take a deep, deep breath.

I lay flat on my face before the Lord, on the hard concrete, for hours until light dawned. No cell mate woke up and no guard came by.

I got in bed with waves of peace washing through my whole body. I slept three hours. When I got up, I was happy. I smiled and asked my cell mates, "How are you?"

They couldn't figure out why I was civil. Thought I was drugged. They asked, "Are you okay? How come you're up so early?"

It was my day off and usually I slept until one o'clock.

"I met God." I told them.

They laughed out loud, "There's no God in prison. Just jail-house religion."

It didn't bother me.

How come? I wondered. But I went into my day, went outside, lifted weights at the weight mat that had all different weights on it, played basketball on teams with four-to-four and went back toward my cell. Russell was coming down the hallway. I walked toward him.

He stepped back.

"What do you want?" he said cautiously.

"Can I go to church with you?"

This was the part where I knew I was healed.

When he shook my hand and I didn't pull away I knew God was healing me—still had miles to go but the process was started. I knew.

"Church tomorrow night at seven. I'll come get you."

"OK."

And I went on to my separate housing unit—upper and lower tiers with ninety men in all.

Next night at 6:58 Russell wasn't there. I hoped he wasn't coming so I wouldn't have to go. I didn't want the inmates to see me going to church. They made you feel weak if you were a Christian 'cause you didn't do the rough stuff like curse, fight, strong arm, make trouble with the staff. Those are the tough things that make inmates feel strong.

At 7:00 sharp, I heard a knock on the window. There was Russell, smiling, waving his hand as he held up his Bible and pointed at it. He got everyone's attention and I felt embarrassed. But I wasn't mad. Actually I was happy. I had to push the button to get the gate open. Over the intercom the guard said, "Whatcha want?"

I tried to whisper it.

Guard said, "Speak up. I can't hear you!"

I had to say it out loud so everyone could hear.

"I'm going to church."

Every face turned my way.

Door opened and I walked out as though I didn't see their stares. Then Russell grabbed me and gave me a side-hug. Put his arm around my neck and hugged me.

I just laughed 'cause I didn't get mad. Felt so good not to get mad.

We went to church. At the end of the service "Pastor Smiley," as they called him, gave an altar call. Pastor had everyone come up so nobody felt embarrassed or singled out.

"Those of you who haven't said the sinner's prayer, there's no better time than now to serve the Lord." Pastor said, "Repeat after me.

God, I am sorry for my sins.

I believe you are Lord

and that you died on the cross for me.

I accept you into my heart.

I know now that I am a new creature in Christ Jesus,

That I am born again.

I thank you Jesus for dying for me.

When the service was over Russell and I were standing in the corner of the room, talking. I wanted his opinion on what happened to me.

"Russell, I want to tell you what happened to me Friday night."

Then I explained it all to him.

"What time did that happen?"

"It started about midnight."

Russell's cheeks flushed, got kinda red. He was blushing and speechless for a while.

"Hey man! What's up?!" I shot my words at him.

"Friday night when you pulled that butcher knife on me, I was so frustrated with you I didn't know what to do. I asked George (his cell mate) if he'd intercede with the almighty God on your behalf with me. In the Bible it says, 'What is bound on earth will be bound in heaven and what is loosed on earth will be loosed in heaven.' We prayed that all the demons that were in you would be bound and cast out and that all your bondage would be loosed. We asked the Holy Spirit to loose you and set you free. At twelve o'clock when you had your encounter with God we were interceding for you."

Russell was crying and that made me cry—first time I ever cried in front of anybody. This time I reached out and gave Russell a big hug instead of him hugging me.

Two weeks later I was baptized in a kiddy pool with green fish pictured on it. I laid back and Pastor Smiley ducked me under. It was out in the prison yard with about 2,000 inmates watching. While they were staring, we were laughing and praising the Lord. That's how I started my life with the Lord. For six more years I was happy and blessed serving the Lord in prison. I had rough times but God always saw me through.

What kind of rough times? I'll tell you one.

About four months after I was saved, it bugged the rough guys because I was different. They started to pick on me. Thought they could strong-arm me 'cause I was weak now, a Christian. Three of them jumped me. Took my head phones, beat me up bad, knocked me out. Split my lip—had three stitches.

Wondered—what I should do? Didn't ask God or my Christian friends. I knew what I had to do.

The next day the guy who took my head phones came outside. I picked up a bar from the weight pile. He had his back to me. I called his name. He turned around, saw me and tried to run, but didn't make it. I whacked him on the head. Knocked him out. The guards got me, put me in lock up. I was in the hole for sixty days. Six by nine foot solitary confinement. But God made it a good time. I had books. Read my Bible a lot and prayed for forgiveness. It was a deep-cleaning-time, just me and Jesus in that tight-fitting cell.

I told God I was afraid I couldn't keep from fighting 'cause the tough guys won't let a non-fighter alone.

God said, "You don't have to worry about the situation I have it under control."

And he sure did.

When I got out of the hole and was outside again, thirty or forty of that big Mexican gang came up to me. I thought I was done. But the leader walked up, stretched out his arm and reached to shake my hand.

"Don't worry. It's over, dude." That's all he said and they all turned and walked away.

That was the end of the big stuff. The little stuff didn't matter.

Now I've been out of prison two years. I go back in a prison ministry and talk to the ones who are interested. I know the ones faking it. I call their bluff. They know I know. I've been there.

Wow! God is good!

# CHAPTER 51

# My Dying Experience

### *Elna Hooker Loudermilk*
### *(Elna is my husband Sam's eldest sister.)*

It was back in 1963 when my husband, Rev. Robert Loudermilk and I were living in Granby, Missouri, pastoring the First Church of God there.

All week I'd been working at "Granby Manufacturing Company," a garment factory.

On Saturday morning I got up and dressed in a mu mu that my navy son sent me from Honolulu.

I felt very tired, so I laid back on my bed. Then I thought of all the Saturday cleaning and the many details of arranging for Sunday church services, so I raised up. A pain struck my chest, neck and head so severely that I screamed out.

My husband came running. He helped me into the living room and onto a recliner. He then rushed to the phone and called our doctor who also had a visiting doctor in his office. Both started for our house immediately. (There was no 911 at that time.)

After this, Robert called out to our neighbour who was standing in his yard. He is a minister and a funeral director. Another minister was visiting with him.

Robert said, "My Sweetheart (that's what he always called me) is very ill. Could you come quick?"

Another neighbour, a male nurse, heard Bob's call. He came rushing. My friend, also a nurse, living two houses away, heard the commotion and came quickly.

The funeral director checked for my pulse and found none. "Preacher, she's gone," he said. Both nurses checked and concurred: "No, there's no pulse."

When the two doctors came and checked me, they agreed: I was dead.

"I'll take her to the funeral home if you want me to, Pastor," the director said.

"No," Robert said, "my wife is not going to a funeral home. She's going to a hospital."

The doctor looked into Robert's face, "Pastor, can't you comprehend? Your wife is dead."

With that, the funeral director said, "It's all right. I'll take her to the hospital. Which hospital do you want me to take her to?"

Robert answered, "To Mc Cune Brooks."

"That's fine," said the director, "I'll take her there and it will save you a lot of money. Her folks live there and that's where you'll want to bury her."

The director brought his pickup truck. He put me on a gurney. He and the male nurse slid the gurney into the pickup. They got into the cab. My friend nurse got in with me. Robert followed in his little red VW. The doctors didn't go. They said I was already dead. Going to the hospital was simply to humor my husband.

All the twenty-three miles to the hospital my nurse friend kept talking to me, kissing me, telling me how much they were going to miss me. I could hear it all and knew what was going on. I comprehended but didn't care. I was wrapped in perfect peace.

As we rode along, dense fog was outside the vehicle. I wondered where it was coming from and decided it was from the gunpowder mill close by. That was the only logical answer I could think of.

When the vehicle turned into the hospital driveway, a very bright light pierced the fog, creating a tunnel through the darkness. Soon I was in the tunnel.

The doctor who stayed back called ahead to our family doctor in Carthage and he, Dr. Wood, was waiting for us at the hospital entrance. When the director wheeled me into the hall, Dr. Wood examined me right there. "She had a massive stroke," he said. "She's gone."

They put me into a private room with a special nurse assigned to stay with me. After a few minutes Dr. Wood left for another call.

The funeral director and nurses left, too.

My husband telephoned two minister friends in Carthage to come pray with him. They brought their wives and the five stood around my bed. Robert quoted Jesus' saying, "Where two or three are gathered together in my name, there am I in the midst."

My Robert was a strong believer in his Lord. He knew Jesus raised people from the dead in New Testament days and Robert believed Jesus would be there with them just as he promised.

As the five encircled me, Robert talked to Jesus. In a simple prayer he told Jesus how much he needed me and asked Jesus to give me back to him. Soon I opened my eyes. Feeling my tongue so stiff and dry, I asked for water.

The nurse gave me a drop. My throat was hard. I couldn't swallow.

Our amazed friends stayed a while, expressed their awe and thankfulness to God and left.

At first, at home, right after the awful pain, I had this incredibly beautiful experience. I felt myself floating upward on the softest air. It was the most comfortable feeling I've ever had. I was totally aware. I could hear the funeral director, the nurses and the doctor arguing with my Robert, trying to convince him that I was dead. That didn't bother me in the least. Rapt in perfect peace and contentment, I was on my way to heaven with not a thought of staying earthbound. Cares left behind; indescribable freedom.

Insulated from all pain, worry or care, I was bathed in quiet happiness.

On the trip to Carthage, there was that fog outside the vehicle. It was like a gray tunnel. Then I was in it, slowly going up toward the light at the end of the tunnel.

When they rolled me into the hospital, I was still in the tunnel. In the hall with Dr. Wood and in the room with the special nurse I was fully aware and heard the din of voices.

After Dr. Wood left and came back he was amazed to find I could move the big toe on my right foot and my right hand fingers.

All the rest of the day and throughout the night Robert sat at my bedside, praying for me. He asked God to make me completely well and normal. After I came back, slowly feeling crept into my body. By morning I had recovered enough to walk. The only vestige of the stroke was that I could not raise my left foot normally and my right hand fingers were stiff. But we went home.

I exercised my foot and my fingers and in three weeks I was walking without the slightest limp. Within a month I was back at church playing the piano for the worship services.

My husband, Rev. Robert Loudermilk, was already highly respected for his loving grace and now even more so for his enduring faith.

It's little wonder.


>Seems to me, God didn't want anyone to deny that Elna really was dead. He had three doctors, three nurses and a funeral director on the scene to validate it. And with the 23 mile trip from Granby to the hospital in Carthage, Missouri she was out of body for over an hour. And that with no brain damage.

I guess prayer brought a miracle that time. A. H.

# CHAPTER 52

# A Pot of Stew

## *A. H.*

I saw Mama praying over everything. I have done the same throughout the years. One of my most miraculous incidents happened over a pot of stew.

It was in our poor days, Sam's and mine, when we had a small church and a very small salary. In those days I still felt sorry for myself over a lot of things. This particular day I was embarrassed and may have had reason for self-pity. A minister and his wife from out of town dropped by to visit us. Sam asked them to stay for dinner. We barely had enough to feed our family of four. Sometimes we ate dry cereal and milk for a week at a time. The children loved it, but I felt sorry for us. Now, again, there was no food in the house to make a presentable dinner. We had no money to run to the store to buy food. How was I going to prepare a dinner for six?

There I sat in the living room with Sam and our guests trying to be friendly while inwardly I was stewing over the idea of company for dinner and nothing to cook. What would I do? What would I say to our guests?

Also, I was seething over the fact that my husband was so inconsiderate of me! Why didn't he check with me before inviting guests to dinner?

I sat and scolded him silently in my mind.

We don't know these people well. If they were close friends, it would be different. We could be forthright with them—even make do with coffee, biscuits and homemade jam.

The opportunity came for me to excuse myself, and leave Sam to entertain the company. I went into the bedroom to pray and to complain to God.

"Sam should have asked me before inviting guests to dinner!" I said emphatically as I knelt in prayer. "Now what can I do? I don't have anything to cook dinner with."

I was hoping God would cause them to leave.

I had more complaining to do, but God interrupted me. He didn't pity me as I wanted him to. He gave me an order instead. His statement shocked me.

"Cook stew."

"Cook stew?" I asked. "I can't cook stew, I don't have anything to make it with."

"Yes, you do," came back in plain language, "You have meat and you have vegetables. Cook stew."

Several years earlier when God did the undo-able for me, I promised I would never say "No" to him again. Obediently, I dried my tears and went to the kitchen. Sneakily, I thought I'd prove God wrong. I knew I didn't have meat nor vegetables to make stew for six people: Sam, the two guests, our two children and myself.

When I went to the refrigerator and drew out the meat tray, there wrapped in a small piece of wax paper lay a tiny piece of hamburger no bigger than a golf ball.

"Humph!" I sneered. "What will that do?"

In the lower part of the refrigerator, in the big, empty, vegetable tray, lay a withered carrot the size of a man's little finger and a quarter of a shrivelled onion. Under the sink in a brown sack lay two small, wrinkled potatoes.

"Make a stew?" my doubting mind asked, "With this garbage?"

"Make a stew."

The words came as emotionless as before.

"—and make biscuits."

Biscuits I can make, I thought. I'm good at that. And we have plenty flour and milk. The children and I will have biscuits and milk. And if I can get Sam's attention maybe he will, too. That should work if I put enough gravy on the these poor-little-scraggly vegetables.

I hoped. But I was far from convinced. Nor was my mind willing to let go of blaming Sam and pitying myself.

When the lady came to help me I assured her my kitchen was too small for both of us. Perhaps she wouldn't mind visiting with Sam and her husband. Actually, I didn't want her to see what I was peeling to put into the stew pot.

A pretty table would help, I reasoned. My best linen and dishes, all wedding gifts, came out of the buffet. In short time we were ready to sit at the dining room table. The stew, with lots of gravy, I put in a medium small bowl so it wouldn't look so skimpy. The tan and white biscuits piled high on a pretty platter, looked ample and even cheery. The children were instructed. But I hadn't had opportunity to inform Sam to eat stew very sparingly.

When our minister-guest asked God to bless the food I said a hearty "Amen." I really meant it! No one else knew how badly we needed God to bless that food!

With trepidation I passed the poor, little, stew bowl and the platter of fluffy biscuits. The guests took normal-sized helpings. I cringed when Sam did, too. However, when the bowl came back to me it didn't seem diminished. I gave the children each a bit and even put a spoonful on my plate. There was still enough to send the bowl around again. Then yet again. The children and I had another portion. Everyone seemed to relish the stew. The biscuits went over big. I couldn't understand how we were all eating our fill.

When all were satisfied and stood to leave the table, the guests thanked me warmly for the delicious meal. To my amazement there was still stew left in that little bowl.

We had leftovers. We really, really did!

****

After this story in brief appeared in *Guideposts Magazine*—"His Mysterious Ways," a lady telephoned me and said the same thing happened in their family during the depression. However, with them it was a bowl of mashed potatoes.

As a child she resented the company that came. A family of four added to their five made nine of them. Knowing the small bowl of mashed potatoes wasn't even enough for their family, why would her mother invite company to stay for dinner? How did her mother expect it to feed them?

"But God provided," my caller said. "He multiplied the small bowl of mashed potatoes and we all had our fill."

I guess Jesus' multiplying four loaves and two fishes to feed five thousand and the widow's oil cruse that kept on running, aren't so far fetched after all.

Oh, for more faith to believe!

# CHAPTER 53

# The Broken Leg

## *Stanley Hoffman*

When serving as a pastor at Carstairs, Alberta, Canada, I joined their church hockey team. The last time I played this rough and tough game was on a team while attending Bible College. But since then my wife Marion and I have served 18 years as missionaries to Africa.

"No opportunity out there to spend time on the ice!" I told Marion. "I do need the exercise and, even though I am the oldest one on the team, I'll give it a try. We play other church teams so it's not going to be all that dangerous. Our night to play is Monday evenings."

I had just prepared a sermon on faith that would take two separate services to deliver. The first part was: "What do we believe?" I deliver this one Sunday morning. Then, Monday night I join the team at the arena.

Now, here I am. It's time to play hockey! I have the puck and when about to slip it into the net, I am knocked to the ice. There are others already sprawled at my feet. My right leg is sandwiched between them and as I fall the bone above my ankle snaps.

We untangle ourselves and I am unable to stand on my injured foot. Is it dislocated, or broken? A couple of team mates help me off the ice. I take off the skate, and not any too soon as the ankle has swollen something terrible. They pray for me and return to the ice, leaving me on the bench.

I try to exercise my faith, after all I had just preached on it. The pain is almost unbearable when I try to stand on the injured leg. It shocks me when Dave, one of the church members, says that I would already be healed if we were still in Africa. I probably would be, come to think of it. But why not here in Canada? Is He not the same here as well? Marion is notified and she comes with the vehicle to take me home. She is hoping that now I will quit the game for good.

All night I am unable to sleep. The pain is excruciating. I end up on the floor. I try several times to walk on it, claiming healing for my leg. Is that not what the Word tells us to do? I give up as the swelling above my ankle appears to be getting worse. In the morning, our daughter Colleen drives me to see the doctor in Olds. The x-ray reveals that my fibula bone is fractured. Before the doctor can put the leg into a cast, he has to force the broken ends back together as they are out of alignment due to my trying to walk on it. Sweat breaks out as he works at it.

The following day, Marion comes for me. I am to be on crutches for six to eight weeks. At home now, the editor of the local newspaper arrives for a picture and article. It appears on the front page a day later. Everyone in town now knows that Rev. Hoffman has broken his leg while playing hockey! As I look at the second part of my sermon that I am to deliver on Sunday, I am tempted to lay it aside for another time. It is entitled: "What do we confess?" I have been confessing healing and nothing has happened! I have searched and searched the Scriptures but to no avail. How can I stand before the congregation and tell them that God answers prayer when you believe and confess? I am not much of an example right now.

Sunday morning comes and I am behind the pulpit. My leg is still in a cast and I am still on crutches. Yes, I preach the second part of my message. The devil has failed to keep me from it. I decide to do it in spite of coming up short. As I share the Word, I am enthralled with it and declare that the next time they see me, I will be without crutches! During the closing song, I suddenly realize what I had just confessed during my sermon! I not only stuck my foot in my mouth, but the cast as well!

With each passing day, I search more fervently than ever Scriptures concerning faith. Tears are shed as I search also my own soul. Why is there no miracle happening? It is now Thursday already! Tonight Marion and Colleen are driving to Calgary to pick up Tim who is flying in from Toronto. As I await their return, I stay awake and continue to communicate with the Lord. Ten days have passed since I broke my leg. I need to be healed before Sunday.

Suddenly there is something resembling an electrical charge that enters the top of my head and continues to pass through my body before exiting at the bottom of my right leg! That's it! I have finally received my healing!

Praise the Lord!

When Marion, Colleen, and Tim arrive back a couple of hours later, I am still awake. I share the wonderful news of my healing. Marion is happy for me. In the morning I plan to see the doctor in order for him to remove the cast. I slide behind the wheel of our car and the cast cracks around the ankle when I reach out to step on the gas pedal! Is the Lord trying to tell me something? That I am to remove it since I no longer need it? I walk back into the house, not an easy feat with a broken cast. We cut it away and I am now back to walking normally. Thank you Jesus! A few days later, I check in with the doctor and tell him what had transpired. He does not say anything. After the examination, he tells me that the foot is all right and not to bother coming back.

Now why did the Lord not heal me any sooner? Why did He make me wait ten days? I can see now, had He healed me at the arena that night, who would have believed I had broken my leg? The team would have said I had only sprained it. It had to appear on the front page of the local newspaper so that as many people as possible would know of it. As well, appearing before the congregation with a cast on my leg also confirmed that I had a broken leg.

There is more to it. It was also a test of my own faith. Would I preach the next part of my sermon? When I passed that test, He had me proclaim in church that I would be healed the next time they see me behind the pulpit! It was also a time of spiritual cleansing on my part, a time for me to build up my faith. And so, He healed me at the proper time. I had persevered, and He then performed the miracle! Hallelujah!

—Stanley Hoffman is a retired missionary to Africa

# CHAPTER 54

# Lost Keys

## *Marion Hoffman*

It is Friday afternoon and time for me to travel the 40 miles to Bomondo Church, in southwest Kenya, Africa, where I have planned a weekend seminar with the women from six congregations. I am leaving Stanley, my husband, at home and taking along Teresa the nurse that works at the Ibeno Mission Hospital, plus Teresa the pastor's wife, and James the area youth leader. We arrive in good time and are invited for tea before the start of the service. I lock the doors on the Landcruiser so none of the children crowding around the vehicle can help themselves to any of the stuff inside.

When it comes time to carry in the material we have brought along for the seminar, I discover that I have lost the keys to the Landcruiser! I go through my pockets again but they are not there. What am I to do now? I ask the Lord for help and the following verse comes to me: "Trust in the Lord with all your heart and lean not onto your own understanding. In all your ways acknowledge Him and He will direct your path." (Proverbs 3:5-6)

The women assist me in searching for the keys. They even look in the outhouse which is nothing more than a deep hole in the ground within an enclosure of grass and sticks. No one finds them. I check the door handles on the vehicle again and am impressed to pound the one on the front left side. When I do, the knob inside pops up! "Praise the Lord!" We are now able to remove the necessary items needed for the meetings.

Finally, the service ends and we ladies prepare for the night. We spread our bedding, we brought along, on the church floor made from mud and polished with cow dung. I again look to the Lord, asking Him for some assurance that He will assist us in getting home Sunday night. He directs me to Hebrews 10:23, "Let us hold fast to the profession of our faith, without wavering for He is faithful that promised." I relax and drop off to sleep, assured that the Lord will either guide someone to help find the keys, or else He will do it in some other way.

In the morning, James approaches me and tells me that he can make it back by tomorrow evening with the spare set of keys that are with the Bwana at the mission, if he can start off immediately. I refuse, and tell him that God will help us to get home. All that day while I am teaching my classes, I walk about as if they are in my pocket. I keep telling the ladies that God will help us get home. In spite of my raising the reward for anyone who finds the lost keys, no one is able to come across them. Children are searching everywhere!

As the day closes, the devil reminds me that when the seminar ends tomorrow afternoon and the keys are still not found, I will really look the fool! I rush into the Word and find assurance in Romans 10:11, "Whosoever believes on Him shall not be ashamed," and in Psalm 31:17, "Let me not be ashamed Lord for I have called upon you." I thank the Lord for His promises and turn in for the night knowing that He will see me through.

Sunday arrives and still no key! But my answer is still the same when asked, "How are you going to get home?"

"The Lord will see us home."

The church is packed with people for the closing service. Many are outside peering through the windows. They have come to see what the white missionary lady will do when it comes time for her to leave. They had heard how she had lost her keys to the vehicle and was telling everyone that God will see her home. They have come to see how He will do it!

In the service the local pastor makes a final appeal for whoever has the keys to step forward and claim the reward. There is no one. Thus the seminar ends and there still is no key for the vehicle! When I, and those who have come with me, walk to the vehicle with our belongings, we discover that all the people have now assembled themselves around the Landcruiser! They want to see the ending to this exciting event. With everyone watching my every move, I lift the hood to see whether I can figure out how to hot wire it.

Stanley would probably know but he isn't here. Afraid I may get a shock, I lower the hood.

What next?

All eyes are on me as I climb inside and sit behind the wheel. It is now time to start the vehicle. I remind the Lord, "The Word has said I will not be ashamed if I trusted in you, and I am now trusting in you fully!"

Someone standing beside the door is jingling something in his pocket. I ask, "Do you have keys?" He said that he is the headmaster of the nearby school and carries the keys for the classroom doors. He hands them to me and I commence to see if one will fit into the ignition. They are either too large or too small until I come to the sixth key. It slides into the ignition and when I turn it, the engine starts! The people are stunned! I slip out of the vehicle, shouting and praising the Lord. I have them gather around and offer up a prayer of thanksgiving for the miracle He has just performed. They all sing the song, "To God Be the Glory," before my group and I start off for home.

When I arrive back at the mission, I relate to my husband all that transpired during the weekend. Upon hearing that the headmaster wants the key back, Stanley tries it himself. If it starts the vehicle, the key will not be returned as he does not want the Landcruiser to disappear while parked unattended in town some day. But when Stanley attempts to start the engine nothing happens, no matter how often he tries. It had worked for me only so that we could get home! A miracle!

The headmaster gets back his key on our next visit to Bomondo

Church. In the service the congregation is asked what they remember about Marion's last trip? They reply that we are to keep trusting the Lord to the very end. This I had done, and thus the Lord was able to use me to teach others about trusting Him as well.

—Marion Hoffman is a retired missionary to Africa

# CHAPTER 55

# Journey of Promise

## *Judy Guyton*

It should have been a time of excitement. A time of dreaming new dreams, making new plans. Making plans for our future—growing old together, taking long walks, planting a rose garden, sitting on the porch, swinging as we talked together and watched the sun go down.

We were excited about moving into our new house. We planned it and watched it day by day as it was being built. We dedicated it to the Lord before one shovel of dirt was ever spaded.

That is—it should have been—a time of excitement.

Two months before we moved into our new home, my strong, vibrant, athletic, intellectual husband of almost 30 years began to have problems. First it was discomfort and blood in Bill's urine. The urologist didn't think it was serious. "Go home, take these pills and come back in three months."

Bill got worse. He became weaker and could hardly do anything to prepare for our move. But we moved with the help of family and friends.

Another urologist diagnosed Bill's condition as an enlarged prostate. Tests, monitoring and medication followed in hopes to reduce the prostate. Bill continued to grow weaker, his pain increased and spread.

One day I was driving down highway I-205, with tears streaming down my face. I called out to God, "My husband is dying and I don't know why and I don't know what to do."

Immediately Psalm 121:1-2 came into my mind. "I will lift my eyes to the hills. Where does my help come from? My help comes from the Lord, the maker of heaven and earth."

In February, 2004, Bill was admitted to the hospital for a simple outpatient procedure. When he was in surgery longer than expected, I knew this was not a "simple procedure."

When the doctor walked into the waiting room, his face told me, "It is not good news." The diagnosis—small cell cancer with the primary site in the bladder and suspicious spots on the liver.

Now the reason for my tears had a name. At least we knew what we were fighting and could start looking for options.

Again my mind went to Psalm 121:1-2. I thought, I can be strong; I can face this; we can face this together. Our faith is strong and we believe in the healing power of God.

Bill was referred to a specialist at OHSU for follow up and possible surgery. At the time, Bill was very weak and complained of pain in his arms and legs. He was admitted and tests were done the next day. It was determined that cancer had spread to the bones. We had to make a quick decision. Would Bill have chemotherapy? Hours could make a difference, we were told.

We decided for chemotherapy. During March, April, and May Bill responded very well. For 6 weeks he felt strong and was able to carry on most normal activities. Our lives were filled with joy and hope.

But unrelenting nausea and vomiting started in July. We made several trips to the Oncology clinic for rehydration and anti-nausea IV's. More tests disclosed that cancer had spread to Bill's brain. Radiation therapy was started immediately, on an outpatient basis.

The last day of radiation therapy when I brought Bill home he collapsed in the garage, getting out of the car. During the next two-weeks

I watched my darling deteriorate. He went from walking, to a walker, to a wheel chair, to losing all use of his legs.

Bill was readmitted to the hospital for more tests. Now the cancer had spread to the spinal cord. He was given two to four weeks to live. With that diagnosis, he was transferred to Hopewell House Hospice Center.

Bill stayed with us for three weeks and then went home to be with his Lord.

\*\*\*\*\*\*

God so graciously gave me some very special gifts during Bill's and my painful journey. The first one was the verses in Psalm 121. I can't begin to tell the number of times I repeated those verses. Over and over and over again I recalled them for a bit of comfort.

People said, "You're so strong. How can you be so strong? I admire your strength." I smiled and said, "Thank you. I'm just taking it one day at a time."

I admit, at first I didn't give God much credit—when talking to others, anyway.

But God was patient with me. Coming home from the Hospice House one night, again I cried out, "God, I'm tired of being strong! I don't want to be strong anymore! Don't make me be strong anymore!"

I heard his soft, gentle voice say, "Judy, I never asked you to be strong. I'm your strength. It's time for you to give me control and remember the promise I gave you."

That was also the night I was finally able to release Bill. I told God, "I love Bill more than I ever thought humanly possible. But even before I knew him, You loved him with a love far greater than I could ever imagine. He's your child. Whatever claim I have on him, I give it up to You."

I've heard others talk about God's peace. But until that moment, I never truly understood that peace which goes beyond any comprehension.

\*\*\*\*\*

Another very rare and precious gift given me was to know in advance the exact date and time Bill would die. This knowledge came in pieces. When he was admitted to the hospital in March, I had a strong impression. It was more than an impression. I actually heard a voice say, "You will have him until September; make good use of the time."

When he responded so well to the chemotherapy, I put that thought out of my mind. Then, when he was admitted to the Hospice House, it came back to me along with this message, "You will have him until the 13th."

Finally, one night when all of his other visitors were gone and we were alone, he asked me if I wanted to be with him when he died. I told him, "Yes. If at all possible I will be here!"

He said, "Then, you need to be here in the early morning hours, because I will leave you at about 5:00 am."

Bill died at precisely 5:00 am on September 13th, 2004.

\*\*\*\*\*

Another gift was given us at the precise time Bill died. I had not told our daughter Bethany of the impressions I'd been given as to the date and time of her father's death. She spent the night with me at the Hospice House that last night. We were one on each side of Bill's bed. Just before 5:00 am, Bethany bent down over her father and said, "Daddy, it's time for you to go home and claim your crown of glory. You've run the race and fought the fight; you don't have to run or fight any more."

Bill took one last breath. His next was in the presence of the Father. I turned to Bethany and said, "We are on holy ground."

I wouldn't have missed that sacred moment for anything on this earth.

\*\*\*\*\*

Another "final gift" was given to Bill and me.

One day when it started to rain, I went out on our patio. There in the eastern sky was a quadruple rainbow, four brilliant bands of color. Bill came out and we stood there amazed at the rare occurrence. Neither of us had ever seen such before—nor have I since.

Bill said, "I want to show you something I read this morning." He opened his Bible to Joshua 23. In this passage, Joshua knows that he is close to death, so he calls the elders together to give them his final words of warning and encouragement. Verse 14 says,

"Now I am about to go the way of all the earth. You know with all your heart and soul that not one of all the good promises the Lord your God gave you has failed. Every promise has been fulfilled; not one has failed."

Bill believed it and so do I. Although circumstances in life can be difficult, challenging, and yes, even disastrous, we can still say, "God is good and He always keeps His promises. Not even the smallest one has failed."

I believe with absolute certainty the promise in Romans 8:28, that in all things God can work for our good.

I wish things had been different. I wish Bill would have lived for many more years. But, because of this journey, I have been given opportunities to reach people and tell my story in ways that never would have been possible. And I believe God will continue to use this. And He will use me for good.

*****

Oh, how many things I have learned through this journey. Practical things, like how to build an entertainment center, how to prepare our taxes, how to work my way through all the paperwork and notifications after a death, how to drain and refill a hot tub.

I have learned to treasure each day, each hour, each moment. I've learned to be independent, to do things for myself and by myself. But, I've also learned how dependent I am on others—how to ask for and accept help. Most of all, I've learned how utterly dependent I am on God.

A great lesson I've learned is that death is nothing to fear. The process may be painful and difficult. The circumstances may be horrible. It may not seem fair and we frequently ask, "Why?" But, death is not defeat;

death is victory. Death is a transition into eternity. Death is the reality of my source of hope.

Too, I have learned to be bold; to take every opportunity to tell others about my Lord. Bill had made a "faith promise" to win 100 people to Christ. A few days before his death he lamented that he hadn't been able to keep that promise. He had only brought 86 people to Christ. I told him I believed God had honored his promise and that he didn't know (yet) what impact he had made on other lives. Who knows, maybe I am to fulfill the rest of that promise.

# CHAPTER 56

# Angels by the Dozen!

## *Samuel Hooker*

(This story is in another of my books, Prayer And Other God Stuff. But so many readers told me they especially liked it, I decided to include it here. You can't help but see God in this —AH)

In my college days angels must have helped me on my way.

When I went to Pacific Bible College, (now Warner Pacific College) I left my '29 Model "A" Ford home with my younger brother, Bob, a high school senior. After my first year, I went home to Carthage, Missouri to see my family and to pick up my car, Huldie. That was my car's name.

On my way back to Portland, Oregon I realized my brother Bob had put some rough miles on the car the year he had it. Poor Huldie's motor kept heating up. I stopped often to let it cool. Twice I had the radiator flushed. It didn't help. When I got to Salina, Kansas I had to fix it. On my limited funds I couldn't go to a garage. I drove around town until I found a wrecking company to get a used radiator. The owner said he didn't think he had one. But I searched and found the exact radiator I needed. I pulled it, paid the man six dollars and left. I drove the car to astraddle a ditch near by, pulled the bad radiator and put the good one on.

I got to thinking of my "hero-brother," Joe, genius mechanic, always messing around with cars in our back yard, he taught me to fix a car. Was he an angel of God for a time like this? Maybe an angel led me to the wrecking yard with the very radiator I needed? If so, that makes two angels.

By the time I had "Huldie" running cool, it was dark. I couldn't afford a motel or to lose more time. I was tired and hungry. But Huldie's repairs ate up my food money. At a grocery store I bought some baloney and a loaf of bread. I made a sandwich and kept moving.

When I reached Twin Falls, Idaho it was midnight again. I knew I could drive to the jail house and get a night's sleep in a cell. It was tempting, but I had to grab a few winks and go on. I'd already lost too much time.

A few miles farther on I heard a strange rattle in Huldie's motor. I got out and lifted the hood. Water spewed everywhere; a busted water pump!

There I was in the dark again. But an angel was there, too. A street light shone on a sign, "Wahl Wrecking Company," with a telephone number, too. Do I dare wake the owner and tell him my sad story? I wondered. With vacation time running out and jobs hard to get, I couldn't lose mine. I mustered the courage to call. He came right down, took me through the yard and found a wrecked car just like mine. Was that the work of another angel?

Mr. Wahl had to be one. At midnight, he got up out of bed, dressed, (He was wearing slippers, no socks.) looked throughout the yard till he found a car like mine and helped me pull both pumps and put the good one on. The price? Two dollars. Saint or angel? Maybe he was both.

Boy! I thought, That's a nice man! I'll bet he's a Christian. I found out later when his son, Sam Wahl, came to Pacific Bible College and we became friends that Mr. Wahl was not only a Christian but a member of the same church denomination I was. How could that happen without Some One bigger than me?

When I left Twin Falls all I had was a little change and a tank full of gas.

It wouldn't get me to Portland. But a couple PBC students who graduated that spring were pastoring one of our churches in La Grande, Oregon. I picked up a hamburger with my last few cents and drove on through the night again.

The Idaho prairies were hot. With my window down, I could hear the sound of rushing water. I wondered, There's no river here. What could that sound be? I stopped to see. It was water in an irrigation ditch. When I went back to Huldie another noise hit my ear. A hissing sound came from Huldie's left front wheel. Down on my knees with my ear to the tire, I heard the stem valve leaking.

Maybe I could fix it if I had wire. There was none in my scanty tool box, but a pair of pliers were. Luckily, a barbed wire fence was nearby. With a prayer of blessing for the dear farmer who put it there, I cut a piece out. With that I wrapped the tire at the stem valve until the hissing stopped.

Was there an angel that made me stop to find out what the running water was, which in turn caused me to hear the hissing tire? If so, that made five. Oh yes, that I was led to stop by a wire fence makes six.

With a prayer and renewed flair for adventure, I was breezing along again, knowing at my next stop were friends who would help me. But when I got to La Grande, I didn't have a dime in my pocket to make a telephone call. Still I went to a phone booth to look up the address of Rev. Harold Lougheed. It wasn't there. The Lougheeds were just starting a church in La Grande, maybe they still met in their home. Maybe they didn't even have a phone. Hungry and broke, I had to find them. Driving from one church to another I asked the where abouts of the "First Church of God" and Rev. Lougheed. No one even heard of them. Frustrated, but broke and hungry, I kept going. After a number of stops a minister said, "Oh yes, I just met Rev. Lougheed at a city minister's meeting Tuesday." He gave me directions. Believe me, I knew he was an angel!

Mrs. Lougheed greeted me with a warm, welcoming smile and took me in. After hearing my sad story she fed me. Knowing it was the only meal I'd have all day, I ate accordingly. Rev. Lougheed took me to the service station and filled my tank with that precious golden stuff they call "gas." He gave me a hearty handshake and off I went.

"Thank You, God!" I said, "two more angels!"

Stomach and gas tank both full, I felt a zesty freedom as I rolled down the highway. I had gas enough to get to Hood River, Oregon. There another couple of PBC students would take me in. I prayed and asked God to see that they were home.

The tall pines of Eastern Oregon got to me. I'd never seen anything like them. Even though the clock was ticking off, I had to stop. In awe, I stood beneath and walked among these giants of nature. Five feet ahead was the first deer I'd ever seen in my life. My it's beautiful, I thought, how can anyone shoot a creature like that?

The forest, with a thick carpet of pine needles, was hauntingly quiet. I'd read stories about Indians in the West. I felt apprehensive. Wonder if there are Indians in here? And I retraced my steps to my comforting pal, good ol' Huldie.

By evening I was in Hood River. No trouble finding the church parsonage, I'd been there before. And God saw to it that my friends were home.

I related my "Ancient Mariner's Tale," thankful someone would listen. Arvella Roper cooked me a good dinner. (I hadn't had anything to eat since the Lougheed breakfast.) They put me up for the night and fed me the next morning. Clarence took me to the gas station.

Her tank full, Huldie perked along happily. I was happy with my stomach full and my destination in sight. I added two angels to my list.

The highway to Portland was scenic, awe inspiring, as it snaked along the mighty Columbia River. Soon we were at PBC, home free! However—

I found out I had one more hidden angel.

When I got out of the car at Pacific Bible college, 2219 S. E. 68th Avenue, I checked my spare tire, curious to see if I could have used it when the valve stem leaked. I tossed the tire out of the wheel well. The under side was completely blown. My rascal brother! He had a flat and didn't repair or replaced it!

Does God have certain angels whose only job it is to look after poor students' tires?

He must have. That one made it an even dozen!

I guess angels can come in dozens. Adele says they can. And she knows about angels. She's collected about two hundred of them.

# CHAPTER 57

# Bullet Shaved!

*Larry Ritthaler*

My father and I often went hunting together. This time we were camping with a group from our church. About ten of us had come to the Malheur National Park near Burns, Oregon to hunt in those beautiful mountains.

On this particular morning I went out with two of my buddies. We went in John's brand new Ford. I was the youngest, fifteen years old, so I sat in the middle. Now we'd been out all day and bagged nothing. We were ready to go back to camp. On getting into the car John said, "Unload your guns and put them in the back seat." I unloaded mind and placed it. Bob, the other kid, did the same.

I don't know why John didn't unload his gun and place it on the back seat. Maybe he thought we'd see a deer on the road and he'd still get his trophy for the day. Instead he handed me his gun. Sitting in the middle, I thoughtlessly put the stock between my legs. The barrel pointed upward. I didn't realize it pointed toward my head. Tired and anxious to get to camp we rolled along at a good clip in John's spiffy new car. All of a sudden the car hit a bump. The gun, jarring on the seat, went off. The barrel sent the bullet up to shave my cheek. The crack was so loud it nearly burst the closed windows and my eardrums. John and Bob lunged out on either side of me. Knowing I shot my face off, I grabbed my head. Blood would be gushing out.

When I came out of my stupor and looked at my hands, they were clean. There was a small hole in the roof of John's new car where the bullet made a clean exit.

Three very shocked and solemn young men drove back to camp. The story stunned the campers. My father lost no time packing up our gear to head for home.

That forever blasted away our father-son hunting trips.

# CHAPTER 58

# A Fat Fuzzy Miracle

## *Karen Siri*

I'm a teacher's assistant in second through sixth grades at Holy Family School. Each year Mrs. Voltz, the head teacher, schedules the study of insects for her spring class. She sends away early for the caterpillar and butterfly larva so the children can watch them develop. This year time got away. She didn't get them ordered. Now the end of the school year was near, there wasn't time to order and have the larva go through the hatching stages.

Mrs. Voltz said, "I hate to do it, but we'll have to skip the insect unit this year. The kids don't know so they'll not be disappointed."

Three of us, Terri Soles, the other assistant, Mrs. Voltz and I were all unhappy about the loss.

"It's such a great unit for the children." Mrs. Voltz said.

On Terri's suggestion, we three took a weekend break and went to Terri's beach house at Rockaway, Oregon.

Sunday morning rather early, Terri and I got up to walk the beach. Mrs.

Voltz slept in. The beach was clean swept by waves. There was not a bit of debris, not even seaweed or the usual rocks. The sand was smooth and silky. Laughing and talking, Terri and I walked together. All of a sudden I looked down. There just in front of me was a round, flat rock. On the rock sat a fat, fuzzy, bright orange and brown caterpillar. I couldn't believe it! Not one other thing was on the beach. But there sat this rock with a caterpillar.

It sat completely still as I picked up the rock.

"Look Terri! A caterpillar!"

"I'm surprised you saw it," she said. "You were talking and looking out at the ocean. How did you happen to look down to notice it?"

I was surprised, too, that I looked down at the exactly, right moment. One more step and I would have missed it.

We were excited! Here was the very thing we were missing for our insect study. We rushed back to the house to show Mrs. Voltz. She was still asleep. But we woke her. We couldn't wait with our miracle-find. She was amazed.

A caterpillar! On the clean washed beach! Not a seaweed, a stone, a tree or a twig. Where did it come from?

We found a container, punched holes in the lid and placed our rare find in it. Mr. caterpillar sat on the rock all the way home. The next morning we took him to his new home, our classroom. The children were excited. Mrs. Voltz told them how this very fuzzy, long, creation of God with its many legs was going to turn into a beautiful, winged butterfly.

The children loved the soft, fuzzy creature. They held it, stroked it, put it on their arms and clothes. It sat where they placed it. Each child wanted a turn with our little, bright orange guest. It was held and loved all day long.

The very next morning, behold there was a hard shelled chrysalis! We didn't have to wait through the larva to caterpillar stage for it to become a chrysalis. Now, would the little creature accommodate us further and grow to be a butterfly while the children were still in class to see? We waited. All week long the children picked up the chrysalis and held it to the light. They could see the butterfly in it.

A week went by and the lack of activity in the chrysalis became boring. The children lost interest. We went to other studies.

Then the last day of school came. In fact it was a half-day. For most of it we were out of the classroom. There was paraliturgy and other activities. When we went back to the class room, just one half hour was left before the children would leave for the summer. Seven-year-old Haley went over and picked up the container.

Behold! There was a beautiful brown and yellow butterfly. We had a miracle. All three of us teachers had shivers; goose bumps ran up our necks.

The children got to see the whole process of transformation as it developed from a fuzzy, creepy, crawly thing-with-legs into a delicate, beautifully winged-flying-thing.

Thanks to God, our insect unit was a success.

Later that day I went to our priest, Father Bob Barricks, and told him we had a miracle. After relating my story, Father said, "You sure did! You had a miracle. I'll have to work that into my homily next September at the first of the school year."

# CHAPTER 59

# "Weird!" or "Wonderful!"

## *A. H.*

"WEIRD!" you will say or "WONDERFUL!" depending on your philosophy of spiritual things. Or you may cast it aside as impossible and untrue. How you look at it is your choice. I happen to believe it is a true story of marvelous spiritual happenings—a wonderful bouquet of miracles!

Before my brother Al's funeral, during the night my sister, Ollie, visited my daughter, Marydith, in her home.

What's so rare about an aunt visiting her niece?

The rarity is in the fact that my sister had been dead for over three years.

"Weird!" you say.

But I must confess, I say, "Wonderful!"

For many years now I have believed that we are just as ignorant of the spiritual dimension before we experience it, as a bird caged from its hatching is of the vast oceans, mountains and high-sunny skies.

As I've said before, three of our family members had near-death, out-of-body experiences. From their testimony and others, over the years I have become an avid believer that the two dimensions—this life and the next, the material and the spiritual—are not that far apart. And so to hear my sane and sensible, then forty-two-year-old daughter share her own, intimate relationship with my very-own-sister was exciting. It's still a thrill to me.

As Marydith related her story to me over the phone, I hurriedly scribbled down every word verbatim. This is what she said.

\*\*\*\*\*

Mama, Ollie visited me last night. Her spirit person told me to make the fruit salad that she used to make and take it to the dinner after the service and to tell the family that I'm bringing it for her and that she will be with us.

Without even questioning, my response was as quick and normal as though Ollie were sitting on the bed beside me. I complained that I had worked in the kitchen for four hours preparing the macaroni salad and cheese cake I was bringing. It was ten o'clock before I was done. And then Joshua (her teen-aged son) came in with one of his demands. We argued about it until it broke into a fight. I even slapped his mouth. When I finally flopped into bed I was exhausted. My sleep was fitful.

At two o'clock I woke up wide and clear. My mind got this message, "Take my sour cream sauce and fruit salad to the dinner tomorrow."

"That's impossible," my mind flashed back. "I don't have the fruit and I don't have the time. I have to leave first thing in the morning to practice the song I'm going to sing."

Her retort came, "You've got the fruit and you can get up earlier."

That's when I said, "Ollie!" 'Cause I knew all the time it was Ollie. I said, "Ollie! I don't have the fruit!"

And then all these little pictures started to pop into my mind of where the fruit was: the bananas that were all black, the watermelon sitting on my kitchen table that I planned to return to the grocery store because the other one I bought with it was all mushy inside, the cantaloupe in the fridge with its dried out, dimpled and leathery skin. It had been in there so long I forgot about it. And the out-of-season strawberries, they're never sweet. Shopping, I picked them up automatically and wondered afterwards why on earth I bought them! I knew we wouldn't eat them.

"That fruit's all garbage," I said.

She said, "Who cares. Make it anyway."

With skepticism I thought, Do you really think I can take this fruit to the dinner and people will actually think they're getting something good?

She goes, "Sure. It'll work." Real light, kinda shrugged her shoulders, "Sure. It'll work."

So I rolled over, set my alarm earlier and thought, Heck, maybe I can get away with it.—and went to sleep. When the alarm rang I woke up excited to make this salad. Ollie was still hanging around. She moved around the kitchen with me, just as she would have before. When I cut the watermelon open sure enough it was pure mush.

"See," I said, "I can't use this."

"Stick your hand in there," Ollie says, "just rake that mush out. You'll feel some firm melon."

So I did. And there were some firm ridges running through the mush. Then I opened up the cantaloupes. They tasted great. The meat was sweet and wonderful. The bananas too, were firm and white inside. So I sliced the fruit and mixed it all together and thought, I wish I had some berries. There's not enough color in here.

Ollie said, "You do. You've got blueberries, raspberries, and blackberries in the freezer."

Her presence by now seemed as natural as if her physical body was there. Sure, I thought, I do. And I remembered that two months ago I made pies and had a couple handfuls left over. I tucked them away.

When I was mixing them all together she said, "Tell everyone 'Hi' for me."

I said, "Ollie! I can't do that! They'll think I'm crazy!"

"Who cares," she says. And she shrugs her shoulders again. "This is for me, not for them."

I still wasn't convinced that I wanted to go out on a limb that far even for Ollie. So I thought, I'll write this on a card and put it by the salad, "Hi everyone from Ollie. This is her fruit salad." That way they could take it any way they wanted without making me a weirdo.

Oh, yes, while I was mixing the salad she said, "Al's here, too."

And I sensed him there. I could feel her turn and pat him on the shoulder. It was like Al was her little brother even though he was older. Of course, he had just arrived. She'd been there longer.

He didn't say a thing. It was like he was absorbing everything and just hanging out with Ollie. It was wonderful to him. But he seemed awed that Ollie was so much still Ollie and that he was still so much himself. He was totally comfortable, but awed at all that was. Quietly and calmly awed.

"Ollie," I said, "why don't you tell Karen (Ollie's daughter) to do this?"

"Karen is too much into her grief," was Ollie's natural reply. "Anyway, if she stood up there and said, "Ollie said to say 'Hi' to everyone, they'd say, 'Poor girl, she's overcome with grief.' Besides, you make that cream sauce so good and Karen can't make it worth a darn. And you're the only person I can tell this to. You're the only one who is open right now."

The feeling I had was that she and Al were gearing up to come to the party. And Ollie wanted to take a dish, too. They were going to be there, she and Al. And then she gave me this thing about Karen. That Karen mustn't grieve so hard. It was real important that Karen know Ollie is constantly aware of them. She sees them and is involved with their lives— all the little, penny ante things with the children. Karen needs to lighten up and giggle more.

"If she could lighten up and giggle with me, her awareness of me would grow stronger." Ollie was instructing me. "I see when the funny things happen and she could laugh with me."

Then she told me she loved it over there.

"The main reason," she said, "was because God has this wonderful sense of humor. Everyone should lighten up because of that.

"He hasn't judged me once," she went on to say. "I've judged myself. I was so heavy on earth. It was a big discovery when I found out how insignificant all those things were that I worried so much about. I looked back and had such remorse about my unkindnesses. But God kept saying, 'It's all right. It's all right. You needed to do that to learn.'"

We conversed the whole time I was making the salad. She tried to tell me as much as she could about it over there.

"We all have connections to our loved ones over here," she told me. "Some do go to another plane. But love-awareness never dies. We're never separated in awareness of each other. Love is an energy that is constant. Energy doesn't end. Just like we're never separated from God because He is love, we can never separate from someone we love."

Before, when I said they'll think I'm crazy if I try to tell them Ollie said, "Hi!" she said, "Oh, they're so dumb about all this—being over here. They'll make a big deal out of it. And it's such a little thing, me telling everyone 'Hi' from here."

She was so cute! She and Al kept hanging around me. Even at the grave side, Ollie wanted me to go over to Karen and tell her not to grieve and to lighten up 'cause Ollie was right there with us all.

And Al was there, too. Oh! he loved the bagpipes! (We had Jason, Anita's grandson play taps at the end of the committal.) Al rode the wind with the high sounding notes. He was all around us and flying high with the music, up over us, viewing the city. I almost opened my mouth and said, "Do you feel Al on the wind with those bagpipes?"

I was crying to see Al so happy. He was soooo happy! The family thought I was crying out of sadness. But I was laughing so hard I was crying—out of joy.

And, oh, Al loves Rita (his wife)! Oh, he loves her! He kept looking at her and saying, "What a woman! What a woman!"

What tickled him so much was that he knew she knew he was with her. I felt the bond. They are mates. They are real mates. And I felt they weren't through. They were together still, sharing their emotional love face to face. And they'll always be together. They are mates eternal. That's what soul mates are.

*****

Now you may wonder about my daughter Marydith, and ask, "Is she stable?"

I can tell you she is a business woman having worked as a teacher and counselor with two different modeling schools. This is the first time in her forty-two years she has ever mentioned such an experience to me. I have never known her to be engaged in any occult experience. Her religion would be considered mainstream.

And you ask, "Did she tell the family 'Hi' for Ollie?"

Of course, she did bring the fruit salad with the scrumptious sour cream sauce. They were both delicious and beautiful in the scooped-out watermelon shell. Her note read, "This is Ollie's fruit salad. Hi everyone."

But that wasn't enough for me. I asked the family for silence. Then I told them Marydith had something to say. I put the melon bowl into her hands to make it as real as possible. Marydith accepted it in good sport. And without batting an eye she gave them a very brief account of Ollie's visitation.

Just as some of you will do, there were those who dismissed it categorically. Others were quizzical. But some, like me, were thrilled and inspired. I think we were in the minority though.

This detailed account Marydith told only to me and my brother Al's wife. I felt it needed to be recorded both for others to read and for me to remember. It instructs me to worry less and to be less judgmental.

"Lighten up," are Ollie's words I'll always remember.

Obviously this is controversial. But I still want to present it as a true happening of my daughter's. Personally, I love it. Maybe all the spiritual facts are not in yet. I can tell you, no one in our family has joined a cult or expanded on this story. But, I would consider it miraculous...a wonder...and a marvel...if this ever happened to me.

(I'm open to it, Lord.)

# CHAPTER 60

# A Tootsie Roll Miracle

## *Fred Hall*

I'm a member of the First Church of God, in Vancouver, Washington. For thirty-six years I sang in a male chorus called, "The King's Choral Ambassadors." And for 26 years I've been a part of the "Live Weekend Teams" that go around the country at our own expense and put on programs for different churches. These teams are made up of lay people who share personal stories of how God affected their lives in significant ways. They may tell how they became Christians. Or any exceptional thing about their spiritual journey. It really is a live weekend when these excited believers share their faith with the people.

"Our congregation has never been the same," is a remark often heard after this group is gone. The love of God and the excitement of "living with the Living God" rubs off on the church people.

At one church a man, a physiologist said, "Before you folks came nobody could have told me I'd be hugging anyone." But I led the team in the little chorus,

God loves you and I love you.
That's the way it should be
God loves you and I love you,
That's the way it will be.

Then I said, "Is it, God loves you and I'm trying to love you, too?' No! It's NOT I'm TRYING to love you. It's I LOVE YOU! Tell someone that and then lay a hug on them if you want to."

Well, by the time the sessions were over, this reserved gentleman, Dr. So and So, was smiling, laughing and hugging everyone around him.

For fifty years I have carried Tootsie Rolls in my pocket to church, six or seven in each pocket. I count on giving away ten or twelve every Sunday after the church service. The reason I started doing this is, if it helps kids to have a more pleasant time at church, maybe they'll want to come more readily. Even if kids just want to come to church to get the candy, at least they will hear about Jesus and maybe give their hearts to him.

One Sunday, after our lunch time, I filled my pockets again. On Wednesday evenings we always have an all-church-dinner. Lots of children attend. Mary and I usually go. This Wednesday I gave out most of my Tootsie Rolls.

Then I went with the "Live weekend" group to Jackson, Mississippi to the Madison First Church of God to do a Live Weekend Program for them.

We usually stay in church members' homes. Friday evening we have a time of singing, prayers and testimonies by the team. Saturday morning we have breakfast and a visit with our host family in their home. We'll share our personal experiences in a more intimate way with the family members. This is always a warm, rich time. At noon we have a lunch together at the church with any of the church people who want to attend. There may be spontaneous sharing there, too. Then we separate into two groups, the men together and the women together. Here we get deeper in our personal sharing. Saturday evening there's another session of songs, prayers and witnessing.

By this time we're more open toward each other. We feel the warmth of God's Spirit of love. We feel we know each other. We're more than acquaintances or friends, we belong to each other. We're brothers and sisters in the great family of God.

This particular Sunday morning when I got ready for church, I put my blazer on. I didn't pay any attention to how much candy I had in the pockets because I wasn't home. I didn't even bring any other Tootsie Rolls. I was just thinking of the talks I'd give at sharing times. Giving candy to children was farthest from my mind.

But then following the second morning service, (This church had two services) I was in the narthex visiting with a young family who had three children. They were like stair steps, two, four, six. Very naturally, I reached in my pocket to give them each a Tootsie Roll. I fished around and found I only had two Tootsie Rolls. There was also a roll of Life Savers. I always carry them to ensure acceptable breath when I'm talking so closely with people as we do on a Live Weekend.

At first I thought, I can't give two of these children a Tootsie Roll and leave one out. So I won't give any. I felt a little bad because I'm so used to giving the children candy. I buy the Tootsie Rolls by the big box and I give them out freely. By now it's a habit. Then I thought, No, I'll give them to the Mama and have her let the children share them. I asked the Mama if it was all right. She agreed. I said to the children, "You're going to have to share these because I only have two Tootsie Rolls."

Then something said to me, "Put your hand in your pocket again."

I did and I had one more Tootsie Roll. I said, "No, you don't have to share them. I have one more Tootsie Roll." And I gave it to them.

By that time a whole group of children saw what was going on and they hurried over, wanting candy. When I saw that, I thought, I'll share the package of Life Savers with them. Then it was like someone said to me, "Put your hands in your pockets." I did. And there were Tootsie Rolls. I started giving these kids Tootsie Rolls. There were at least seven or eight kids. I gave them each a Tootsie Roll and I still had more.

When I went into the lunch room for our dinner I felt impressed to stand up and share this miracle. At first I thought, Oh! This is a miracle. But I can't tell it. No one would ever believe me. But then—why should I care if they believe me or not. I can hardly believe it myself. But I know it happened. I was there! It happened to me! And I stood up and told the Sunday dinner group what just took place. After I related the account, I said, "Does anyone want a miracle Tootsie Roll?" Several people held up their hands. I reached into my pockets and pulled out two hands full of Tootsie Rolls. I tossed a Tootsie Roll to each person with a hand up. I don't know how many there were. But I still had Tootsie Rolls in my pocket after that.

At the airport, when the team left Jackson, I hung my blazer in my clothes bag, zipped the bag up, folded it over and checked it through. I always travel light.

When we got to Portland, Oregon I was at the baggage claim waiting for my bag to come around. A call came over the loud speaker asking Fred Hall to come to the claims office. When I went in they told me the machinery had chewed up my bag. There in a box lay my snarled clothes: shirt, pants, blazer, under things, notebook, etc. Everything was chewed on. The workers and I went through the box of stuff and assessed the damage. I checked my blazer and sure enough, there were still two handfuls of Tootsie Rolls in the pockets. I left everything else but my note book and the Tootsie Rolls.

The woman attendant told me to go shopping and replace everything. It so happened I hit a good sale and was able to buy a jacket, 2 shirts, and a pair of trousers for $150. I didn't buy anything else, underclothes and such, because I didn't need them. When I took the receipts back to the claims office the attendant gave me $150 for the clothes and $25 for the wardrobe bag.

I put the "Miracle Tootsie Rolls," about ten or twelve, in my new jacket and took them to my Wednesday evening church dinner. There I told my story and gave the Tootsie Rolls to the children.

I just can't believe God would be that good to me. I don't deserve it.

# CHAPTER 61

# Over Many Seas

## *A. H.*

In 1960, as we drove west on highway 80 in Wyoming, I looked out the side window of the car so my husband, Sam, wouldn't see the tears streaming down my face. I was praying, "Oh God, are you taking us out into the wilderness to die?"

We left our secure nest in Muskogee, Oklahoma because, pray hard as we did, we couldn't get away from the strong feeling that it was God's will that we go to pastor the Woodstock Church of God in Portland, Oregon. All the stress of making the hard decision, preparing for the move and finally pulling up deep roots kicked up Sam's old mysterious malady. He was so sick and exhausted before we left, that his good friend, Dr. Don Bernamonti, put him in the hospital for three days.

As a youngster, Sam was run over by a car and dragged in front of the back wheels for thirty feet. When he gained consciousness he reached up to touch his hurting head and his skull fell in. Although he surprised the doctors by gaining use of his limbs and mind, he was plagued ever after with times of debilitating headaches, blackouts, numbness and excruciating pain throughout his whole body.

Sights became sounds growing so loud he could hardly bear it. And looking at his arm, instead of seeing a normal limb, it would appear the size of a toothpick. Sometimes in his disorientation he would get lost and have to wait until the attack was over before he could find his way home.

Now, here we were, far from home, stressed out, sick and confused, not knowing when he would black out.

Sam said, "I'll not make it to Oregon. I'll die on the way."

I didn't know but what he would. Besides the fact that I loved him, I had three children to raise alone if he left us.

My mood was dark enough from leaving all we had built up through the years: our good friends, the home we worked so hard for and the financial security Sam gained through his industrial chaplaincy to say nothing of the church we loved so dearly and had served for eleven years.

To think we were going to a lot of strangers and to a big city we always said we wouldn't live in. To top it all, Sam might be incapacitated or non-existent. All this filled my mind with enveloping, black clouds of fear and despair. Stress brought these attacks on Sam. And here we were, in one of the most stressful situations of our lives.

I feared the worst.

Nobody knew our problem. We kept the secret even from our children. Sam was careful not to let the church know. He didn't want the inevitable attention it would bring. But I could tell the Lord. And I did, with groanings that could not be uttered. Now I was telling him in tears and great pain of heart.

It was then I heard these words which I could never forget.

"Cannot I, who have brought him to you over many seas, not even keep him unto you?"

These were not words of my making. I don't talk like that. They did not come out of my head. They came into my head from outside the window. I heard them in my ear. I knew they were not audible to Sam.

I mused over them.

Yes. God did bring us together over many seas. Sam's parents had their roots in England, Ireland, Scotland and Germany. His forefathers sailed many seas to bring him to his birthplace in Carthage, Missouri. He, himself, crossed mountains, rivers and deserts to come from Carthage, Missouri to Portland, Oregon.

My great grandparents migrated from Germany to Russia where my mother and father were born and grew up. As a couple, my parents crossed the Atlantic Ocean to Canada and from there came to Portland, Oregon. My mother's dream of a great and bloody war in Europe and hearing God's voice say, "Go to America" was the only reason I was in this wonderful land and in proximity to meet my Sam.

Feeling a call to the ministry, Sam came to Portland to attend Pacific Bible College, now Warner Pacific College. I felt called to the mission field and enrolled in this college. Although we grew up two thousand miles apart, we were sitting in classrooms together.

We found each other.

Surely God figured in that. Now he was letting me know that he still figured in where we were and what we were doing.

I took heart. Sam endured. We made it!

Although we went through struggles, we have had, at this time, forty-six years of wonderful ministry in Oregon. We have made a multitude of friends and been privileged to live close to my family members on the West Coast. We prayed with and for them and have often been called on for help. We've officiated at eight of their funerals. Now the rest of the family tells us we can't die because we haven't finished our job. Although there is only one sibling other than myself living, there is still a lot of family: children, grandchildren, nephews and nieces to pray for and to help.

Hard as it was to leave all behind and come to Portland, I believe God brought us here especially for my family. I'm glad he did. He, who "brought us together over many seas," has kept us together in good health and happiness for 64 plus years.

I praise him.

# CHAPTER 62

# A 60-Year Secret

## *Adele Hooker*

Sam and I carried a secret for sixty years. We didn't want the troubling situation to interfere with our church ministry. And we didn't want our children to be worried or insecure, so we never shared with them or anyone else. Now that our days of responsibility to others are over (ha-ha) we can let the cat, with it's many litters, out of the bag.

I must say, I have marveled at Sam's tenacity and integrity.

*****

The story has to start at Sammy's early school days. Too, it starts with Fourth of July firecrackers.

When Sammy was eight years old he was coming out of his grade school class. Meandering along the playground, he spotted his older brother across the street, shooting off firecrackers. Oh, this little excited boy loved his big brother Joe, but the most exciting thing was Joe had firecrackers! Sammy darted across the street. No, he started to.

He darted into the street.

Jamey Wyatt was driving past the school to show off his new Model A Ford. He was rolling along at a good clip when Sammy ran out.

You guessed it.

There was a bang, The car hit a little boy. The boy fell in front of the car. The front wheel of the car ran over him. The boy was caught in front of the back wheel. For thirty feet and over a train track the boy's body rolled like a tube in front of the rear wheel.

Sammy's body was mangled.

Joe pulled his little brother out from under Jamey's car. A kind man driving by stopped, put the broken boy into his car, took him to Sammy's house and laid him on a couch in the living room.

The doctor came. There was no examination. None was needed. There was no hope for the mangled body.

But Sammy's parents were praying people and they had a church full of praying people. Every day friends stopped by to pray for Sammy.

For two days Sammy was comatose. The third day he awoke. His head hurt and he reached up to feel it. His hand pushed his skull in.

The first thing Sammy saw and heard was Joe kneeling at his bedside praying,

"Dear God, please don't let Sammy die."

Well, the story has to move on.

Sammy didn't die. But the doctor warned his parents that he would be paralyzed.

During the year of missed school, friends and church members came to see Sammy. Some brought small gifts. Jamey's mother, Mrs. Wyatt, brought a large bowl of eggs, probably three dozen. No doubt she expressed her sorrow. That was the only visit from any of the Wyatt family Sam remembers. Jamey never came.

One of the church friends was P. J. Smart. He had only one arm. Joe told Sammy that kids kept bothering P. J. asking how he lost his arm. P. J. said, "I'll tell you once if you promise never to ask again." They promised.

P. J. said, "It was bit off." Of course, then the kids were more curious than ever. P. J. held them to their promise.

P. J. Smart was smart. He brought things to interest Sammy. One thing Sammy will never forget was the red racer, a six inch long, metal car that P. J. set right on Sammy's chest. Sammy couldn't reach out to play with it but, oh! he could see it. And he could smell it. Sammy never forgot that metallic smell. It awakened the urge to get well. He wanted to play with his new, shiny red car.

That was good therapy before we ever heard the word "therapy." The doctor too was interested in physical therapy. He came to the house and had Sammy move his arms and legs. He helped Sammy stand, then walk and urged him to throw things. In time, the doctor took Sammy outside and had him throw rocks. It was a great day when Sammy could throw a rock and hit the telephone pole.

The doctor told his parents that it was nothing medical science did. A higher power was responsible.

Sammy recovered, but not fully.

He didn't die. But many times he wished he had. His headaches were near unbearable. His vision played tricks on him. Some sights became sounds so loud he'd nearly go out of his head. At times he'd lift up his arm to shield his eyes from the light and his arm appeared the size of a tooth pick. Year after year he was plagued with pain and weird suffering that made him think he was insane. Finally he decided everyone lived with the same problems. He just had to endure.

Quietly and patiently he endured—secretly, too.

It was several years after we were married before I learned Sam's bitter secret. Here it is.

We were living in Tacoma, Washington, pastoring the First Church of God there. Sam was out visiting the sick. At one point, he told me later, that he sat in the car thinking, I'm out here visiting the sick, but actually, I'm sicker than they are.

Sam said his hands were numb. He couldn't feel the steering wheel. He hit his face—couldn't feel the touch. I'd better go home, but I don't know which way is home. I'll go to that service station and ask them.

When he got to the service station he couldn't talk. He mumbled, incoherently, turned and drove away. He kept driving. Soon he found himself in front of his house.

That night was our Wednesday prayer meeting. We attended. Sam was on the platform, at the pulpit. I saw he was having trouble. Soon he said, "I'm sorry but I'm sick. I have to go home. I'm going to ask my wife if she will come and take over for me."

I did.

When I got home Sam was in bed. I said, "What's the matter, Honey?"

"I can't talk. I hurt all over. You can talk to me but don't ask me any questions. I can't think."

From then on we pursued a medical course. We saw doctor after doctor, went to clinic after clinic. For many years no medical help was forthcoming. All doctors were mystified.

Sam's sister "Bertie" worked as a medical secretary at the army hospital in Memphis, Tennessee. We contacted her, told her about Sam, asked if she might consult the doctors there for advice. She made arrangements for us to come to Memphis and for Sam to be examined by those doctors.

The first examination with all the head tabs and wires to monitors brought forth nothing. Then one of the doctor's said, "Wait! I have an idea."

They put Sam to sleep. Physical therapists worked Sam's arms and legs hard until they had Sam exhausted. His brain waves went wild.

"Ah! that's it!" the doctor exclaimed, "It's stress."

The only medication they had for Sam was a bottle of amphetamines. Bertie got them from the hospital pharmacy. He was to take the pills daily. Which he did for a while. But he couldn't reconcile with the decision to live on drugs for the rest of his life. He flushed the pills down the toilet and resigned himself to live a life of pain and struggle.

By this time we had moved to pastor the Church of God in Muskogee, Oklahoma, USA.

Here I became plagued with a constant cough. It never let up, day or night. I tried everything. Every doctor I went to told me I had a cold. In disgust I felt like saying, "Thanks a lot, but give me back my five dollars (the doctor's fee at that time) I could have told you I had a cold before I came."

One morning I got down on the floor on my hands and knees before God—I had already prayed until I was utterly discouraged. In silence I screamed my prayer to God. "Please God, please God, please help me. I'm exhausted. I can't breathe. I can hardly work to care for my family. Please, please, please help me!"

I don't know how long I was there begging God when I heard these words, "Go to doctor Brown Oldham."

When Sam got home I told him I was going to see Dr. Brown Oldham.

"No you're not. He's an alcoholic and a woman chaser. You can go to any doctor you want. I'll even take you to Tulsa (50 miles from Muskogee). But you're not going to Brown Oldham."

"I'm sorry, Honey," I said. "But I was praying so hard when I felt I heard God say, 'Go to Dr. Brown Oldham.' I know he's not a moral man, but I'm not going to him for moral advice. I'm going to him for his medical knowledge. And you know he has a good reputation as a medical doctor."

I went to Dr. Oldham and he helped me—allergies.

I told doctor about Sam. He said, "Have him come in."

I went in with Sam. I heard doctor tell Sam that his work was his problem. "It's a stressful job like mine. But you can't tell your people to go to hell, like I can. And that's your problem. Change your work to a less stressful job."

"I don't think I can, Doctor. You see, I feel I've been called to do this."

Oldham understood.

"Then there are two things you can do. One, control your emotions. Don't let yourself get high or low. Two, go home in the middle of the day, take a shower if you need to, put your pajamas on and go to bed just like you would at night. Cut your day in two. That's your prescription. Now you're your own doctor. No one can help you but you."

This is what Sam lived with. This is how he endured. Although he didn't take it quite as far as Dr. Oldham advised, Sam did try to take a nap during the day, which was often impossible.

As for pressure: Sometimes we had a funeral in the morning, a dinner with the family in the afternoon and a wedding in the evening—not conducive to naps.

I've marveled that Sam could keep a good sense of humor. He's known to be a joker and a good storyteller. Once a little boy sitting on the front bench in church said to his friend, "You'll like pastor's sermon, he tells good jokes."

Sam's friend of sixty-five-years, Bill Taylor, told me, "Sam adds spice to life."

Our school-teacher-grandson Nick said, "Pop is the most of all an integritous man" (meaning, adhering to moral and ethical principles). I must agree.

I've heard Randy laud his father for humility.

I laud him for his faithfulness to our marriage and our family and for the good pastor I knew him to be—also for the fact that he never complains of having to clean up a cat mess or carry out the garbage.

Sam's struggles helped him to understand others and to be compassionate. In every church we pastored he was a peacemaker. A returned missionary from China, Belle Watson, once said to me, as she stood shaking her head, "He has heavenly wisdom. He has heavenly wisdom."

Another time, a man who gave pastors a lot of trouble, dropped his head as he went out of the sanctuary and mumbled these words, "I guess you can teach me something after all."

After nearly eighteen years of pastoring the Woodstock Church of God in Portland, Oregon, the congregation needed to expand their building facilities. This was the third time we needed to do so. Sam felt he could take on a limited project. But some of the younger board members wanted a total relocation and building program with a fund-raising-drive. Sam resigned.

Although people were shocked and most didn't understand, Sam never explained. He never revealed his secret. "That's work for a younger man," is all he said.

I was shocked, too. I loved our church. When I questioned Sam's decision he said, "That would kill me."

It was no doubt wisdom. We engaged ourselves in the less stressful interim ministry. We served churches while they were in pastoral transition. With Sam's understanding, he was able to help each church secure a fine pastor.

Today Sam may be farther from dead than ever. He's 87, in reasonably good health, able to put in a full day's work, six days a week, keeping up our home and property. He fixes everything except my computer. He won't touch that.

Although less, Sam still struggles.

Not many Sundays ago we were on our way to church. When we got there Sam said, "Honey, I have to go home. (He didn't add, "and go to bed.") You go on in. I'll come get you after the service."

At times when I want to do a certain thing Sam may say, "I couldn't do that at all. But you go ahead."

Why the secret all these years?

1. Neither one of us thought Sam would live long. I went back to college to receive my teaching certification so I'd have income to support our family.

2. We didn't want to worry our children or have them feel insecure as they grew up. They're grown now with families of their own.

3. Sam didn't want the church to worry about their pastor.

4. Sam never wanted to be the center of attention. He didn't want people concerned about him. He wanted to be on equal terms.

The Apostle Paul told Timothy to "endure hardship as a good soldier of Jesus Christ" (II Tim. 2:3).

That's what Sam has done.

I decided to dedicate this book to Sam, then tell his story in the last chapter. I told him, "You're going to be the alpha and the omega of my book—the beginning and the end."

Sam laughed.